French
FUN

An exciting visit to the everyday language of our Québécois friends and neighbours

D0721737

Steve Timmins

Illustrated by Keith O'Donnell

Northwinds Press/*Les éditions Vents du Nord*
P.O. Box 391, Belœil, Québec, J3G 5S9
Telephone: (514) 467-0654

Typeset, printed and bound in Canada by
Imprimerie d'éditions Marquis ltée

ISBN 0-9696345-0-1

Dépôt légal/4ᵉ trimestre 1992
Bibliothèque nationale du Québec
National Library of Canada

Cover design by Werner Arnold

Illustrated by Keith O'Donnell

Illustration concepts by Steve Timmins and Keith O'Donnell

Mille fois merci! A thousand thanks!

I would like to thank the following people for their invaluable support and assistance: Carole Laprise, André Raymond, Michel English, Alain Chalifour, Susan Cohen, Marie Rochon, Arnaud Anquetil, Terry Murray, Linda Robitaille, Jean Bellefleur, Jean Beaulieu, Diane Tétreault, Dorothy Eber, Peter Jensen, Paul Jensen, Joan Folinsbee, Becky Timmins, Gretchen Timmins, Anne Synnestvedt-Timmins, Marc Lacourcière, Gilbert Taggart, Laurent Santerre, Jany Hogue, Henri Grenon, Harvey Chang, Claude Tremblay, Serge Tanguay, Michael Folinsbee, Peggy Dean, Hubert Maisonneuve, Jane Broderick, Nicole Girard, Guy Camirand, Thomas McElreavy, Michel Mascolo, Colette Leblanc, Dominique Ménard, Nabil Saad, Pierre Robert, Cheryl Watt, Debbie Stupple, Marvin Miller and all the folks at Landmark Education.

CONTENTS

INTRODUCTION

FRENCH IN THE AIR!

There's French in the air in good old Québec! From chic Montréal out to rugged Gaspé and historic Québec City north to Laurentian forests, it's like a song and is everywhere to be heard. *Mais oui!* It's that distinctive French tongue — a unique mix of Old World tradition and New World spirit — that has flourished in Québec for almost four hundred years and remains the leading lady of Québec's vibrant French culture.

French Fun seeks to capture some of this magic and put it within easy reach of English-speaking Canadians and Americans wishing to communicate more effectively with their French-speaking neighbours and to have better access to Québécois theatre and song.

This book is a selection of words, phrases and other features of everyday French as spoken by francophones all across Québec in every walk of life. Many of the entries are words you must know in order to understand Québec French in everyday situations. Others are an essential part of your Québécois vocabulary when you want to communicate on a more personal and intimate level with your francophone friends or when you simply want to inject a little life into your daily French conversations.

Listed in dictionary form for easy reading, the entries include common Québécois words like "**Souper**" (six o'clock dinner) and "**Jaser**" (to make conversation), as well as exclamations and interjections to express your feelings and opinions: "**Je t'aime!**" (I love you!), "**T'es tannant**" (You're a pain in the neck) and "**C'est super!**" (It's great!). You'll also meet some of those elusive short forms that shoot past at the speed of light in fast conversation, like "**Y**" (pronounced "ee" and short for *il* — he, it) and "**C't'une**" (pronounced "stoon" and short for *c'est une* — it is).

Other entries give you the typical Québécois pronunciation of certain words and sounds such as "**P'tit**" (pronunciation of *petit*) and "**Dz**" (pronunciation of the consonant *d*). There are colourful words and expressions galore, including "**Fou comme un balai**" (crazy like a broom) and "**Vite sur ses patins**" (fast on one's skates). They are all explained and matched up with their English equivalents.

Topping off the list are words such as "**Chansonnier**" (a Québécois folksinger) with a special cultural dimension, and "**Anglicisme**" (anglicism) which denotes a linguistic reality close to all Québec francophones. The accompanying descriptions will give English-speaking Canadians and Americans greater insight into these interesting elements of Québec culture and shed some light on how French Québecers feel about their language.

School French programs in English Canada have evolved over the years and are now placing more emphasis on Québec and Canadian French, rather than serving a strict diet of far-away Parisian. This guide thus aims to reinforce the trend towards greater recognition of Canada's own French language and to provide anglophone Canadians with French words and expressions that really work in Québec.

It is important to note that some of the French words heard every day in Québec and considered typical Québécois speech are shared with the French people of France, making these words part of what is called "international French". A number of entries fall into this category: "**Voyons!**" (Look here!), "**Quoi de neuf?**" (What's new?) and "**Bon vivant**" (a fun-loving person) are just a few. While international in scope, they are an integral component of everyday Québec French and a necessary part of your Québécois vocabulary.

The tone of this book is intentionally light-hearted, with the focus zooming in on the personal and colourful side of Québec French, all with a view to putting a little pizazz into that much-too-serious business of learning a second language. And why not! — when anglophone Canadians can have more fun than a barrel of monkeys translating their favourite expressions into real Québécois equivalents and popping off snappy French phrases left, right and centre!

The French language is an everyday reality for almost all Québec anglophones. Many have a good working knowledge of it; others are brilliantly fluent. Still others are grappling daily with the language or are hesitant to get their bilingual feet wet. **French Fun** is written especially for you — to provide invaluable support in your efforts to communicate effectively in French for career success and for greater freedom to participate fully in all aspects of Québec life. More importantly, this book is intended to ''crash the sound barrier'' so you can get out there and make whoopee with our fun-loving French-speaking partners.

For English-speaking Canadians outside Québec who don't often get the chance to practise their French, having a few Québécois expressions up your sleeve and a little knowledge of Québec culture can help break the ice when visiting or doing business in *la belle province*. Moreover, **French Fun** offers you an insider's look at the real French of Québec and is the perfect point of departure for your further discovery of the many facets of Québec's blossoming French culture.

Our American friends, especially those who visit Québec for business or pleasure and those who live in states that receive flocks of Québec tourists, can enjoy the cultural experience this guide has to offer and will find it surprisingly useful for making conversation with their new Québécois friends and acquaintances.

All in all, **French Fun** is written to bring you closer to Québec French and the people who speak it, for more effective communication, more *bonne entente* and one heck of a good time speaking French in Québec!

Bonne chance et bon dialogue!

THE STORY OF QUÉBEC FRENCH

The first Frenchman to come to the New World was Jacques Cartier, who discovered the St. Lawrence River in 1535 and explored inland to the impassable Lachine rapids. Then came Samuel de Champlain, who founded the first permanent settlement at Québec City in 1608, starting a century-long wave of French colonization.

The settlers of the colony emigrated from all the old provinces of northwest France. Most came from Normandy, Île-de-France (Paris), Poitou, Aunis, Saintonge and Perche. They spoke their various provincial patois, which reflected the situation in France in the 17th and 18th centuries when many dialects were spoken and the dialect of one province was often not understood by the natives of another.

The colonists worked closely together to survive in the wilderness, and, despite the many patois, a common language soon emerged: the Île-de-France dialect prevailed to become the only dialect spoken in the colony by 1700; a limited number of words, however, were preserved from the other patois. One theory for this is that although the settlers from Île-de-France were not the largest group, their dialect was the most widespread, as many of the newcomers spoke it as a second language.

Hence, within less than a century, a language evolved to form the basic mold of the French we hear spoken in Canada and Québec today. Canadian French, in fact, can be traced back to this period with amazing precision: studies show that the majority of Canada's French population is descended from the fewer than ten thousand original colonists who settled in New France between 1608 and 1700.

By the middle of the 18th century, New France was a bustling colony of seventy thousand inhabitants, most of whom were native-born, and who identified strongly with their New World home and their own French tongue.

The final rupture with the language of France came with the signing of the Treaty of Paris in 1763, under which New France was transferred from French to British rule. Thenceforth, Québec French evolved in even greater isolation, little influenced by the major linguistic events taking place in France that were shaping Parisian French into its present form. Interestingly, the Île-de-France dialect that had become the French language of the colony also rose to prominence in France — through its own path of evolution — to become the standard French of France.

After 1763, English became the main language of administration in the colony and the confederation. Québec French was influenced by the English language of first the British and later that of English Canadians and Americans. For the next two centuries, industry and commerce in Québec operated mostly in English, deepening the impact of the English language on spoken and written French.

Over the same period, a great number of Québec francophones emigrated south to the United States and west to Ontario and the Prairies — which explains the similarity of accent among most French-speaking Canadians.*

An important development in the evolution of Québec French was the gradual re-establishment of cultural ties with France, beginning effectively in the 1870s. French as it had evolved in France then became an ongoing influence on the language, though of minor importance until much later.

In the 1950s, Parisian French, with its international prestige, became the standard for Canada's CBC French radio network.

Québec's Quiet Revolution of the 1960s brought about heightened interest in language among the general francophone population and gave unprecedented momentum to social change and cultural

---

* The Acadian French spoken in the Maritimes is an exception. The origins of Acadian French are mainly south of the Loire River in France.

11

development in Québec. A flow of creative energy from Québécois writers, singers and film-makers helped carve out a distinct Québécois literature, song style and film genre. School reform and greater contact with the language of France added further dimension to the evolution of Québec French during this period.

To this day, Québec French is influenced by the French of France: Parisian French grammar is taught as a standard in Québec schools; through modern communications, cinema and travel, Québec francophones are increasingly exposed to the dialect of their French "cousins" abroad, and communication with France, for commercial or other reasons, usually requires adapting to the vocabulary of the larger group.

English, too, as the most widely-used language in North America and the world's lingua franca, continues to make an imprint on the French language of Québec. While extensive English usage by francophones adds a unique quality to the language, its influence is such that a major challenge for future generations may be to keep Québec French alive and relevant in our fast-paced global cultures.

QUÉBEC FRENCH TODAY

The melody of Québec French varies boldly from the sounds of France. While Parisian French enjoys great prestige, our home-spun variety has authentic charm and a character all its own, profoundly shaped by its North American experience. This character shows in the particular way our Québécois friends have of pronouncing, intonating and giving rhythm to their words and in a body of French vocabulary that is unique to Québec. Included in this vocabulary are new words describing Canadian reality, some words taken from Amerindian languages and numerous words adapted and borrowed from English. Most fascinating of all is the oral tradition preserved from 17th-century

France: many words, meanings and pronunciations long since lost in France are still heard daily in contemporary Québec French.

While Québec French is distinct, it is not a language unto itself, but a common tongue shared with the French-speaking world. It is to French French what Canadian English is to British. Common roots in the Île-de-France dialect, a shared system of French grammar and the enormous range of vocabulary that all French dialects have in common allow for ease of communication and cultural exchange between Québec and other francophone peoples.

Overall, Québec French is quite homogeneous throughout the province. Each region, however, boasts its own typical expressions and distinctive features of pronunciation. Québec francophones, like their English Canadian and American neighbours, prefer a style of speech that is natural and direct, personal and familiar — no doubt the result of a common New World heritage. Resonant and sensual, spoken Québec French is often music to the ears. And when uttered from the lips of the most polished Québécois speakers — who concoct a special blend of Québec and Parisian flavours — it is some of the most eloquent and exquisite French anywhere to be heard!

USING THE WORD LIST

French Fun is written in dictionary form for easy reference. Carefully reading this section will help you understand how the entries work and enable you to derive the most benefit from them.

PRESENTATION

Entries are presented generally as follows, with some variations in form.

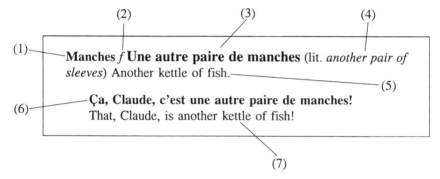

Legend

1. One of the main words of the expression under which the entry is listed. When a main word begins an expression, as in **Français de France**, the expression itself will be smack up against the margin.

2. The masculine or feminine gender of a noun.

3. The word or expression itself.

4. A literal translation to enlighten and entertain the reader.*

5. A Canadian English equivalent or a translation showing the meaning of the word or expression. A word or expression may have several meanings, which are determined by the context and the speaker's tone of voice.

* Note: Keep in mind that English expressions like *another kettle of fish* sound just as hilarious when translated literally into French. Where the expression is the same in both languages, the English translation is automatically a literal one, e.g., **Chauffeur du dimanche** Sunday driver.

14

6. An example of how the entry may fit into typical, everyday French speech. These examples offer additional vocabulary and show how to put words together the way the Québécois do in natural speech.

7. A translation of the example into everyday English.

SPECIAL FEATURES

Entries may be longer or shorter than the above example; some entries will give you additional information about a word, expression or other feature of spoken Québec French including **(a)** pronunciation, **(b)** origin and **(c)** a synonym or variation that is part of international French but also used in Québec and possibly more familiar to students of French as a second language. Example:

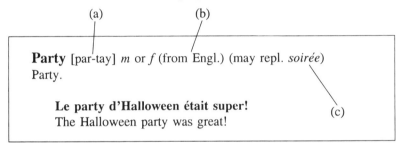

(a)   (b)

Party [par-tay] *m* or *f* (from Engl.) (may repl. *soirée*) Party.

Le party d'Halloween était super!
The Halloween party was great!

(c)

Other entries, such as **Vous vs. tu** and **Boîte à chansons**, include comments on the use, background and significance of the term.

PRONUNCIATION

The approximate French pronunciation is indicated for words whose pronunciation is not generally included in standard dictionaries, or when especially useful. The following symbols are used:

Vowels

[a]	as in hat
[ay]	as in say
[aw]	as in saw
[e]	as in get
[ee]	as in bee
[ī]	as in Hi!
[i]	as in kit

[o]	as in go
[oo]	as in too
[ew]	for the fabulous French *u* as in *tu*; to achieve this sound, say "ee" while rounding your lips.
[oy]	as in joy
[u]	as in but
[uu]	as in good
[uh]	this sounds like [uu] and [ew] said quickly one after the other and blended together

Consonants

The pronunciation of most consonants is obvious. Some that must be defined:

[n]	as in win
[j]	a soft *j* sound, similar to the *s* in leisure
[r]	There are two *r* sounds in Québec: the rolled *r* and the Parisian-style *r* gras-sayé; for beginners, the English *r* will do fine.
[s]	as in sun
[z]	as in zest

Nasal Sound

| [ñ] | represents the French nasal sound as found at the end of *bon* and *vin* — similar to the nasal sound in the English "un hun" (yes). |

ABBREVIATIONS

m	masculine noun
f	feminine noun
repl.	replace, replaces
var.	variation
pron.	pronounced
lit.	literally means
iron.	ironic (that which means the opposite of what it states)
inf.	a word that lends itself to informal rather than formal conversation; not indicated where the English translation is also informal.
**	very informal or slang; not indicated where the English equivalent is also very informal. While this level of language is sometimes to be avoided, like the informal level, it is essential to the vitality of a living language.

16

A NOTE ON SHORT FORMS

The short forms in this book such as "**C't'une**" and "**Y**" are part of natural speech in Québec. This tendency to shorten words and word groups is not unique to Québec, but also common in English and other languages.

Students of French as a second language must be able to recognize and understand all the short forms they hear, but may choose to stay with the textbook forms when speaking French until they have developed one solid line of patter and can switch from short to full forms with consistent ease.

A NOTE ON PUNCTUATION

The punctuation in the French sentence examples throughout the word list is designed to represent smooth, flowing speech and is not intended as a guide for standard punctuation in written French.

WORD LIST A to Z

A

À [a] (inf.) (may repl. *ce* before *matin* and *soir*) This.

> **Il fait beau à matin.** (instead of *ce matin*)
> It's nice out this morning.
>
> **Elle sort avec Jules à soir.** (instead of *ce soir*)
> She's going out with Jules tonight.

À [a] (inf.) (may repl. *de*) Denotes relationship, possession.

> **La fille à Georges.** (instead of *la fille de Georges*)
> George's daughter.

Achaler To bug.

> **Achale-moi pas!**
> Don't bug me!

Accrocher ses patins (lit. *to hang up one's skates*) To resign, retire, take one's leave.

> **Après 30 ans comme maire de Montréal, le légendaire Jean Drapeau a accroché ses patins.**
> After 30 years as Mayor of Montréal, the legendary Jean Drapeau retired.

Après 30 ans comme maire de Montréal, le légendaire Jean Drapeau a accroché ses patins.
After 30 years as Mayor of Montréal, the legendary Jean Drapeau retired.

See Accrocher ses patins

Adonner (inf.) (may repl. *arriver*) To happen, to be possible.

Use *ça* as the subject of the verb *adonner*.

> **Ça nous a pas adonné d'aller à la plage.**
> We didn't happen to/weren't able to go to the beach.

Si ça adonne If one gets around to it, if one has the chance.

> **Je vais le réparer si ça adonne.**
> I'll fix it if I get a chance.

Affaire(s) *f* Thing(s), activities, business.

You need to know this staple of Québec conversation and the many ways it's used. Here are some of the most common:

Affaire (may repl. *chose*) Thing.

> **Où as-tu mis mes affaires?**
> Where did you put my things?

Être d'affaires To be good in business.

> **On dit que vous êtes d'affaires.**
> They say you're good in business.

Faire l'affaire To do, to do the trick.

> **Ça fera l'affaire!**
> That'll do the trick!

Faire son affaire (inf.) To suit someone, to be okay with someone.

> **J'irai si ça fait mon affaire.**
> I'll go if it suits me.

Est-ce que ça fait ton affaire si j'amène ma mère?
Is it okay with you if I bring my mother along?

Homme, femme d'affaires *m,f* Businessman, businesswoman.

L'avoir l'affaire (inf.) To have the knack, to have what it takes.

Il l'a l'affaire!
He's got the knack!

Mêle-toi de tes affaires! Mind your own business!

Ne pas avoir d'affaire à (inf.) To have no business.

T'as pas d'affaire à parler à ma blonde!
You've got no darn business talking to my girlfriend!

Petite affaire Bit, wee bit.

Juste une petite affaire, s'il te plaît.
Just a wee bit, please.

Son affaire (inf.) One's business, situation, problem, or whatever one is doing.

Il connaît son affaire!
He knows his stuff!

Comment ça va, ton affaire?
How's that project of yours coming along?

Aimer! *To like* or *to love*, that is the question!

"Je t'aime!" said the young Québécois to the Saskatoon filly. Now how in Sam Hill was she supposed to know if he was talkin' romantic or just friendly-like? Didn't she learn in school that *aimer* meant both like and love?

Je t'aime!
I love you!

See Aimer

To be sure, it does mean both. But luckily, you can usually determine the speaker's feelings by keeping a close look-out for the way in which *aimer* is said and for the decisive little modifiers that may get tacked on behind to water it down.

> **Je t'aime!**
> I love you! (especially when uttered with real warmth and/or
> breathiness)

> **Je t'aime bien.**
> I like you.

> **Je t'aime beaucoup.** *or* **Je t'aime ben gros.** (inf.)
> I like you a lot.

Aimer (quelque chose) To like, to enjoy something.

> **J'ai beaucoup aimé mon voyage en Gaspésie.**
> I really enjoyed my trip to the Gaspé.

Air Fais de l'air! (lit. *make like the air and blow*) Get lost!

> **Eh, fais de l'air, toi!**
> Scram!

See JOUER

Aise *f* **Être à l'aise** To be at ease, to be well-off.

> **Sa famille est très à l'aise.**
> His family is very well-off.

J'ai beaucoup aimé mon voyage en Gaspésie.
I really enjoyed my trip to the Gaspé.

See Aimer (quelque chose)

Aller S'en aller A familiar sound to Québécois ears, *s'en aller* often replaces the basic French verbs *aller* (to go) and *partir* (to leave).

> **Nicole s'en va à Vancouver.**
> Nicole's going to Vancouver.

> **Bon, je m'en vais!**
> Well, I'm off!

See VENIR, S'EN

Allô! (inf.)(may°repl. *bonjour*) Hello! Hi!

> **Allô Suzanne, t'as l'air en forme!**
> Hi Sue, you're looking well!

Allure *f* **Avoir de l'allure** (inf.) (may repl. *avoir du sens*) To make a lot of sense, to seem like a good idea.

Use *ça* as the subject.

> **Ça a beaucoup d'allure!**
> That's one heck of an idea!

> **Ça a pas d'allure.**
> That doesn't make sense.

Ami,e *m,f* Often means *boyfriend* or *girlfriend*, as well as just plain old *friend*. To tell which, listen to how it's used and to who's doing the talking.

> **L'amie de Jean-Jacques.**
> J.J.'s girlfriend.

26

Elle est "mon" amie.
She's my girlfriend.

Elle est juste "une" amie.
She's just a friend (not my girlfriend).

Petit,e ami,e (lit. *little friend*) Boyfriend, girlfriend.

Comment va ta petite amie?
How's your girlfriend doing?

Amour *m* Love, darling (for ladies, gents and kids).

Oui, mon amour!
Yes my love!

T'es un amour!
You're a darling!

Ange *m* **Être aux anges** (lit. *to be with the angels*) To be in seventh heaven.

Pierre est aux anges!
Pete's in seventh heaven!

Anglais,e *m,f* Here's looking at you kid! This is the Québécois term for you, the reader — if you're an English-speaking Canadian, that is. In the larger sense, it covers anyone whose mother tongue is English, including our American neighbours and the British. But in the Québec context, it more often than not refers to English-speaking Canadians.

C'est un Anglais.
He's English-speaking.

27

Pierre est aux anges!
(*Pierre's with the angels*)
Pete's in seventh heaven!

See Anges

Ma femme est anglaise.
My wife is English.

For Canadians who have adopted English as their first working language and prefer a more generic term to describe themselves, *anglophone* or a specific reference to their cultural background such as *Canadien allemand* (German Canadian) or *Canadien italien* (Italian Canadian) will do fine.

Anglicisme *m* Anglicism.

Ho hum. Snoozzz. Yawnnn. Well, what looks here like a puffed-up piece of linguistic academia, or real dullsville, is actually an everyday word that most Québécois know by heart!

Simply defined, an anglicism is *any English word used in French*, and you will encounter them daily when conversing in Québec.

Some examples:

Anglicism	French word it may replace
le waiter	le serveur
les brakes (auto)	les freins
un building	un bâtiment
un show	un spectacle
les boys	les gars
un meeting	une réunion
le boss	le patron

There are also other kinds of anglicisms — variations on the same theme — which have to do with French word meanings and grammar that have been influenced by English. But to make a long story short, we won't elaborate on these here.

Anglicisms abound in the French of Québec and are often more familiar friends to Québécois speakers than the French words they replace or that were never typically employed in Québec. It's not such a surprising phenomenon when you stop to consider the North American context where this small francophone population lives amid a vast English-speaking world and given the fact that industry and commerce in Québec operated mostly in English from the 1760s to the 1960s.

French Québecers have been in continual contact with the British, Americans and English Canadians and are constantly exposed to English language and culture through business, the workplace, product labels, big league sports, television, radio, magazines and books. As enriching as this may be, it makes it hard for Québec francophones not to incorporate into their own language the many English words they have come to know.

Looking to France, we see the same trend occurring, although to a much lesser degree. Fond of American culture, the French of France use numerous English words in their daily speech, even where Québec francophones use French ones, e.g., France: *shopping* (Québec: *magasinage*), France: *weekend* (Québec: *fin de semaine*) and France: *hit parade* (Québec: *palmarès*).

The general attitude of Québec francophones today is that anglicisms are overused and that many should go — especially the ones that obscure communication, are inelegant or have common French equivalents. Unfortunately, some Québécois educators have been over-zealous in their attempts to remove most anglicisms from the language, deeming them *fautifs* (incorrect) based on no sound linguistic reasoning. But the language will continue to evolve, and anglicisms will eventually either fade out of use or become accepted into the language based mainly on their utility.

Many popular anglicisms, like *fun, jogging* and *leadership*, have been indelibly woven into the fabric of Québécois culture and are as inseparable from their language as *bon voyage* and *déjà vu* are from Canadian English.

Appartement *m* (lit. *apartment*) (inf.) From old French, may be heard in the sense of *room*, replacing *pièce*, which is confusing, but helpful to know when you're out there apartment-hunting.

> **Il y a trois appartements ici.**
> There are three rooms here.

Après (lit. *after*) 1. (inf.) May follow *fâcher, crier* and *attendre*.

> **Le patron est fâché après lui.**
> The boss is mad at him.

> **Crie pas après moi bonhomme, c'est pas ma faute!**
> Don't yell at me bub, it's not my fault!

> **Elle attend toujours après Lise.**
> She's always waiting for Lisa.

For formal speech, use *fâché contre*, drop *après moi* after *crier* and use *attendre* without *après*.

2. (inf.) (may repl. *être en train de*) To be in the process of.

> **Elle est après faire son travail.**
> She's (in the process of) doing her work.

Argent *m* Money

> **Faire de l'argent comme de l'eau** (lit. *to make money like water*) To make lots of money, to really rake it in.

> **L'argent lui brûle dans les mains** (lit. *money burns in his hands*) He's a spendthrift. He can't hold onto his money.

> **L'argent pousse pas dans les arbres** Money doesn't grow on trees.

See PIASSE; SOUS; TOMATES

L'argent lui brûle dans les mains.
(*Money burns in his hands*)
He's a spendthrift. He can't hold onto his money.

See Argent

Arrête (donc)! Stop! Cut it out! Come off it!

> **J'ai eu 100 % dans tous mes examens. — Arrête donc!**
> I got 100 percent on all my exams. — Come off it!

See VOYONS DONC

Assiette *f* **Ne pas être dans son assiette** (lit. *to not be in one's dish*)
To not be one's old self.

> **T'es pas dans ton assiette aujourd'hui Philippe!**
> You're not your old self today Phil!

Avoir (lit. *to have*) To get, to beat, to trick.

> **Tu m'as eu!**
> You got me!

Avoir, Chercher, Trouver (lit. *to have, to look for, to find*) Verbs typical of spoken Québec French to express the English idiom *get*.

(avoir)   **J'ai eu un billet pour excès de vitesse.**
I got a speeding ticket.

(chercher)   **François est parti chercher du pop-corn.**
Francis has gone to get some popcorn.

(trouver)   **Où as-tu trouvé cette belle antiquité?**
Where did you get this beautiful antique?

"But what about *obtenir* and *procurer*?" some readers may ask — ah ha! Well, these reflect standard written Québec French and are a little more highfalutin than what is usually encountered in everyday speech, much like the English equivalents *obtain* and *acquire*. Use *obtenir* and *procurer* for formal speech, and *avoir, chercher* and *trouver* for normal conversation.

33

Awaille! [a-way] or [a-wī] ** (from the verb *awailler*, var. of *envoyer* — to send) Hurry up! Move it! Let's go!

> **Awaille Albert! On va manquer le train!**
> Move it Albert! We're going to miss the train!

See VAS-Y

Ayoille! [ī-yoy] Ouch! Yikes! Wow!

> **Ayoille, ça fait mal!**
> Ouch, that hurts!

> **Ayoille! Le professeur a l'air furieux.**
> Yikes! The teacher looks furious.

> **Ayoille, c'est super!**
> Wow that's great!

AYOILLE!
(OUCH!)

AYOILLE!
(WOW!)

AYOILLE!
(YIKES!)

B

Bavard,e *m,f* Big-mouth, windbag.

> **Réjean est le bavard de la classe.**
> Reggy is the big-mouth of the class.

See LANGUE

Beau, belle Most English-speaking Canadians know these French adjectives mean *beautiful*. Elementary my dear Watson! But what they often don't discover until they get right into the thick of French conversation is that these modifiers are also equivalent to *nice* as used to casually describe things and events (though not considered as informal as *nice* in this sense).

> **Carole a passé une belle fin de semaine.**
> Carol had a nice weekend.

> **C'est un beau travail.**
> That's a nice piece of work.

> **T'as une belle voiture.**
> You've got a nice car.

C'est beau! In keeping with the above description, this phrase means *it's beautiful*, or *it's nice*, but is also used in Québec as a synonym for *that's okay*.

> **C'est beau!**
> That's okay!

See CORRECT; O.K.

Beau, bon, pas cher! (lit. *nice, good, not expensive*) A great buy! A snappy comment you can make about your latest purchases, all the while boasting about your shrewd shopping savvy.

> **Ça, c'est beau, bon, pas cher!**
> That's a great buy!

Beaucoup beaucoup (inf.) (repetition for emphasis or as a style of speech) A lot.

> **Y avait-il beaucoup de monde au concert de Roch Voisine?**
> **— Oh oui, beaucoup beaucoup.**
> Were there a lot of people at the Roch Voisine concert? — Sure were, one heck of a lot.

Other words typically repeated include *ben ben, très très, fort fort, toutte toutte*, and from TV advertising *c'est sûr c'est sûr c'est sûr!*

Bébite [bay-beet] *f* (inf.) Bug, small animal, bug in computer program.

> **Il y a encore quelques bébites dans le programme.**
> There are still a few bugs in the program.

> For human bugs see ACHALER; TANNANT

Bec *m* (lit. *beak*) (usu. repl. *baiser*) Kiss.

> **Donne-moi un gros bec!**
> Give me a big kiss!

In Québec, friendly kissing means double duty. You always kiss twice, placing one kiss on each cheek.

Beigne *m,f* (lit. *doughnut*) Nitwit, klutz.

> **Je suis un vrai beigne au volley-ball.**   (*une vraie beigne*
> I'm a real klutz at volleyball.   for women)

Note: to pronounce this correctly, start with "bing" as in Bing Crosby, then shift it slightly to [beng].

Belle *f* **T'en as fait une belle!** (lit. *you did a beauty*) Great play Shakespeare! Way d'a go!(sarcastic)

> See BRAVO

Ben [bañ] (inf.) (var. of *bien*) Really, a whole lot.

> **T'es ben beau.**
> You look really nice.

**   **J'ai ben de l'argent.**
> I've got loads of money.

   Ben oui! (often repl. *mais oui*) Of course!

   Ben là ... Well, as far as that's concerned....

> See BIEN

Ben gros (inf.) (may repl. *beaucoup*) Lots, a whole lot.

> **Elle a besoin de ben gros d'affection.**
> She needs lots of affection.

38

Best [bes] *m* (inf.) (from Engl.) The best, the best thing to do, the greatest.

Des vacances dans le sud, ça c'est le best!
A holiday in the south is the greatest!

Bête (lit. *beast*) Stupid, abusive, ignorant.

Que je suis bête!
How stupid of me!

Nathalie a été bête avec lui, elle lui a parlé d'un ton bête.
Natalie was abusive with him, she talked to him in an abusive tone.

C'est bête ce que t'as fait.
That was an ignorant thing to do.

Rester bête (inf.) (lit. *to stay beastly*) To be very surprised, to be taken aback.

Gérard est resté bête quand je lui ai annoncé la nouvelle.
Gerry was flabbergasted when I told him the news.

Bien A popular little number that gets fantastic mileage in everyday dialogue.

1. Very.

Odette est bien fatiguée.
Odette is very tired.

2. Well.

    Je le connais bien.
    I know him well.

3. Well....

    Bien, qu'est-ce que t'en penses?
    Well, what do you think?

4. Comfortable.

    T'as l'air bien dans ce fauteuil.
    You look comfortable in that armchair.

5. In certain contexts *bien* may be packed with all sorts of meaning that can't be expressed with just one modifier in English.

Consider:

    Jean-Pierre est bien avec elle.
    Jean-Pierre is happy, at ease, gets along well with her.

    Nous sommes bien ici.
    We are comfortable, well-off and just downright happy being here.

6. **C'est bien!** That's good! That's nice!

A phrase for your repertoire of conversational fillers, or it may serve specifically to pat your speaker on the back or be used to express a certain contentment.

    J'ai eu le contrat. — C'est bien!
    I got the contract. — That's good!

    Elle a adoré ton cadeau. — C'est bien.
    She loved your gift. — That's nice.

7. **Avoir bien été** To have gone well, to have been enjoyable.

You'll hear this short phrase in questions from francophone friends concerning your trips and other fascinating experiences. It sounds best with *ça* as the subject of the phrase.

> **Puis ton voyage à Toronto, est-ce que ça a bien été?**
> So how was your trip to Toronto?

> **Ça a très bien été!**
> Very nice!

Bienvenue (influenced by Engl., may repl. *de rien, je vous en prie*) You're welcome.

> **Merci pour ton aide Stéphane. — Bienvenue.**
> Thanks for your help Steve. — You're welcome.

Bloc *m* (inf.) (may repl. *immeuble*) Apartment block, building.

> **Voilà mon bloc.**
> There's my apartment building.

Bloc *m* (lit. *block*) (inf.) Head, noggin.

Avoir un mal de bloc (lit. *to have a sore block*) To have a headache, to have a hangover.

> **Jean-Luc avait un gros mal de bloc ce matin.**
> Jean-Luc had a bad hangover this morning.

Blonde *f* (inf.) Girlfriend (regardless of hair colour!).

> **C'est ma blonde.**
> She's my girlfriend.

See AMI,E

Bobo *m* (kiddie talk) Any bump, bruise or scratch that hurts or is apparent.

> **J'ai un bobo ici maman!**
> I got a bump here mummy!

Boîte à chansons *f* (lit. *song box*) The *boîtes à chansons* were small entertainment rooms off the regular commercial circuit, that featured young Québec folksingers, or *chansonniers*, as they were called. The rooms flourished in Québec from the mid-1950s to late 1960s and gave these new-style Québécois singers a platform for their music and poetry. Indeed, many important Québec singers made their start here. Moreover, the proliferation of the *boîtes à chansons* across the province was symbolic of an exciting cultural renaissance known as the *Révolution tranquille* (The Quiet Revolution). The haunt of students, artists and journalists, the *boîtes à chansons* were characterized by their intimacy, lively ambiance and simple decor, akin to the coffee houses of English Canada. Fortunately, today, for connoisseurs of Québec culture, some modern-day *boîtes à chansons* evoke the era through their decor and live music, offering a mixture of old and new Québec song styles. Look for them in Old Montréal and Old Québec City.

See CHANSONNIERS

Reference: The Encyclopedia of Music in Canada

Bon, bonne Good (masculine and feminine forms) Have a nice... Enjoy your.... In everyday speech, you can say these before almost everything to wish people well at whatever they are about to do.

> **Bon appétit!** Enjoy your meal!
>
> **Bon voyage!** Have a good trip!
>
> **Bon match!** Enjoy the game!

Bon travail! Enjoy your work! Hope your work goes well!

Bonne journée! Have a nice day!

Bonne semaine! Have a good week!

Bon Être bon pour (lit. *to be good for*) (inf.) To be available, to be able to make it. For women say: **Être bonne pour**.

>**Eh François, es-tu bon pour vendredi?**
>Hey Frank, can you make it on Friday?

Bonhomme *m* (lit. *good man*) Guy, pal, buster. Refers usually to an adult male. In some cases *bonhomme* may mean *husband* or *father*. See here how it's used, first in a friendly, then an antagonistic way.

>**Ce bonhomme-là, il est extraordinaire! Il a acheté des dindes pour tout le monde à Noël.**
>That guy is incredible! He bought turkeys for everyone at Christmas.

>**Écoute bonhomme, enlève ton auto ou je serai pas capable de partir!**
>Listen buster, move your car or I won't be able to get out!

See GARS

Bonhomme sept-heures *m* (lit. *seven o'clock man*) Québec bogeyman.

From the bone setter* of Québec's early days and the fear inspired by his visits evolved the name and legend of the dreaded *bonhomme sept-heures*. He's an imaginary ogre that exasperated parents may evoke to scare their unruly kids off to bed or to incite them to be in on time. As the story goes, any stragglers still up or outside after the hour of seven

Le bonhomme sept-heures
(The seven o'clock man)
Bogeyman

will be snatched up and stolen away by this black-eyed monster — or he may throw (not sprinkle) sand in their eyes, like a kind of demented Sandman.

Directions: Powerful stuff. Use only for real hard cases. Scares the pants off them.

* The bone setter travelled around setting broken and dislocated bones. Notice the closeness in sound between *bone setter* and *bonhomme sept-heures*. Hmmmmmmmm!

Bonjour! Hello! *or* Goodbye! While the French of France say *bonjour* as only a greeting, our Québécois chums say it as both a greeting and farewell, depending on whether one is coming or going.

Bon sujet *m* (lit. *good subject*) An interesting person.

> **Paul est un bon sujet.**
> Paul's an interesting guy.

Bon vivant *m* One who lives on the lighter side, has *la joie de vivre* and likes feasting and good company.

> **Félix est un bon vivant.**
> Felix is a merry old soul.

Bouger Ça bouge! (lit. *it's moving*) That's where the action is, there's a lot of action.

> **Ça bouge au centre-ville!**
> Downtown's where the action is!

Bout *m* Area, district, part of town.

> **C'est dans quel bout, l'endroit que tu cherches?**
> The place you're looking for is in what part of town?

> **Tu restes dans quel bout?**
> Whereabouts do you live?

See COIN

Bout de temps *m* A while, a little while.

> **Suzanne est restée un bout de temps dans les Laurentides.**
> Susan lived in the Laurentians for a while.

> **Je vais me reposer un bout de temps.**
> I'm going to rest up a bit.

Boutte [buut] *m* ** (var. of *bout*) See BOUT

Branché,e (lit. *plugged in*) Said of someone who is onto something good, who has got it together or who is with it.

> **Hervé est branché, il fonce dans son cours d'écologie.**
> Harvey's onto something good, he's really into his ecology course.

> **Elle est branchée.**
> She's with it.

> **Branche-toi!**
> Get with it!

Ça bouge au centre-ville!
Downtown's where the action is!

See Bouger

Bras *m* **C'est sur mon bras** (lit. *it's on my arm*) It's on me, it's my treat.

> **C'est sur mon bras les gars!**
> It's my treat guys!

Brasserie [bras-ree] *f* A beer and beverage room with decor ranging from very simple to trendy. Watch out! You may confuse its pronunciation with that of *brassière* [bras-ee-yayr] — a women's undergarment.

Bravo! Hurray! Way d'a go!

> **Bravo, c'était une excellente performance!**
> Hurray, that was an excellent performance!

> **Bravo, idiot, t'as brisé ma bicyclette!**
> Way d'a go, idiot, you broke my bicycle!

See BELLE, T'EN A FAIT UNE

48

C

Ça (repl. *cela, ceci*) This, that, it. Heard often in everyday conversation.

> **Qu'est-ce que tu penses de ça?**
> What do you think of that?

> **J'aime ça!**
> I like it!

C'est ça! That's it! That's right!

> **Pour aller à Sherbrooke, je prends l'autoroute 10? — C'est ça!**
> To get to Sherbrooke, do I take Highway 10? — That's right!

Cabane à sucre *f* (lit. *sugar cabin*) Traditionally, rustic buildings set deep in the woods, the *cabanes à sucre* were built for the production of maple syrup and sugar. Still, like a rite of spring during *le temps des sucres*, Québecers flock to these rural places to partake of the sweets and commune with nature. Of the thousands of *cabanes à sucre* that exist, many are private. Others are not so romantically situated, but are designed to seat hundreds for some real whomp up *parties de sucre*. Overall, the *cabanes à sucre* and the tradition of harvesting maple syrup are considered a valuable economic and cultural heritage in Québec.

Cadeau *m* **C'est pas un cadeau!** (lit. *it's not a gift*) It's no treat! It's no laughing matter!

> **Robert a une mauvaise grippe depuis une semaine, et c'est pas un cadeau!**
> Rob's been down with the flu for a week, and it's sure no treat!

Cabane à sucre

Café *m* **Un café attend pas l'autre** (lit. *one coffee does not wait for the other*) One coffee right after the other.

A good expression for the office, where this timeless brew is consumed by the gallon.

> **Est-ce qu'il boit beaucoup de café? — Oh oui, oh oui, un café attend pas l'autre!**
> Does he drink a lot of coffee? — Oh yes, oh yes, one right after the other!

Capoté,e [ka-puu-tay] Nuts, off one's rocker.

> **T'es capoté!**
> You're nuts!

See SAUTÉ

Cassé,e (lit. *broken*) (inf.) Broke, out of money.

Cassé comme un clou (lit. *broken like a nail*) Flat broke.

> **Je peux pas t'amener au bal Monique, je suis cassé comme un clou.**
> I can't take you to the prom Monica, I'm flat broke.

Casser Se casser la tête (lit. *to break one's head*) To rack one's brain, to worry oneself to death.

> **Casse-toi pas la tête pour ça!**
> Don't worry yourself to death over that!

51

Un café attend pas l'autre.
(*One coffee does not wait for the other*)
One coffee right after the other.

See Café

Certain! For sure! Definitely!

> **As-tu vu la pièce Broue? — Certain! Tout le monde l'a vue.**
> Did you see the play Broue? — For sure! Everyone's seen it.

Chaleureux,-se Warm, friendly, hospitable.

> **Les gens d'ici sont très chaleureux.**
> Folks here are really friendly.

Chance *f* **C'est une chance!** or **Une chance!** It's a lucky thing!

> **Ils vont baisser les impôts cette année. — C'est une chance!**
> They're lowering taxes this year. — It's a lucky thing!

C'est une chance is often pronounced *c't'une chance* [stoon shawñs].

See C'T'UNE

Chanceux! Lucky you! (for a man). To address a woman, say **Chanceuse!**

Chanson de fête Birthday song. See FÊTE

Chansonnier *m* Québécois folksinger-poet. Most notably, the young singer-poets of the 1960s who played the *boîtes à chansons* and broke with the status quo of imported French and American song styles. Québec greats Félix Leclerc, Gilles Vigneault and Jean-Pierre Ferland, among others, emerged from the ranks of this new generation of *chansonniers* to become heroes of Québec's cultural revolution. The *chansonniers* of the 60s performed alone, accompanying themselves on

53

guitar or piano, playing their own compositions and singing about human values, patrimony and society. This trend eventually gave way to *chansonnier* groups (Jim & Bertrand) and groups that reflected merging folk and commercial streams (Harmonium). In brief, the 1960s generation of *chansonniers* was important for both its social role and the impetus it gave to the development and promotion of a truly Québécois song style.

See BOÎTE À CHANSONS

References: Encyclopedia of Music in Canada
              La chanson québécoise

Chanter la pomme (lit. *to sing of apples*) To sweet talk, to flirt.

> **Luc te chantait la pomme, tu sais.**
> Luke was flirting with you, you know.

Chapeau *m* **Parler à travers son chapeau** To talk through one's hat.

> **Georges parle à travers son chapeau, il est pas bien informé.**
> George is talking through his hat, he's not very well informed.

Char *m* ** (may repl. *auto, voiture*) Car.

> **Bon, où est-ce que j'ai stationné mon char?**
> Now, where did I park my car?

Chat *m* **Il y a pas un chat** (lit. *there isn't a cat*) There isn't a soul.

> **C'est tranquille ici, il y a pas un chat.**
> It's quiet here, there isn't a soul.

54

Chauffeur du dimanche *m* Sunday driver.

Checker [che-kay] (inf.) (from Engl., may repl. *vérifier*) To check, to look over.

Checke ben ça! Look at this! *or* Check it out!

Chemises *f* **Les chemises de l'archiduchesse, sont-elles sèches ou archi-sèches?** (lit. *are the archduchess's shirts dry or super-dry?*) A common tongue-twister that's hard to say without flubbing the *ch*'s and the *s*'s. Perfect for demonstrating your second-language skills when you dash it off nonchalantly at earth-shattering speed!

By way of cultural exchange, you may suggest *She sells seashells by the seashore* or *Peter Piper picked a peck of pickled peppers.*

Chez nous 1. (lit. *our place*) Is sometimes said figuratively in the sense of *chez moi* — *my place* by one person living alone.

Viens chez nous.
Come over to my place.

2. *Our home* in the larger sense of town, region, province, country, or *back home, where I come from.*

Après son voyage, Jean était content de revenir chez nous.
After his trip, John was happy to be back home in Québec.

C'est une fille de chez nous.
She's a girl from back home.

Chic 1. Trendy, chic.

> **C'est chic, ta nouvelle robe!**
> Your new dress is very trendy!

2. Nice.

> **C'est chic de ta part.**
> That's really nice of you.

Chicane *f* Argument, arguing, quarrelling.

> **J'aime pas la chicane!**
> I don't like arguments!

Chicaner Se chicaner To argue, to quarrel.

> **Ils se chicanent tous les jours.**
> They quarrel every day.

Chien *m* **Avoir du chien** (lit. *to have some of the dog in you*) To have guts, to have a strong personality.

> **Elle a du chien!**
> She's a dynamo!

Choqué,e (lit. *shocked*) (inf.) Really mad, steamed.

> **J'étais choqué quand j'ai vu ma note finale!**
> I was really steamed when I saw my final mark!

Elle a du chien!
(*She's got some of the dog in her*)
She's a dynamo!

See Chien

Chose *f* (lit. *thing*) (inf.) What's-his-name, you, buster.

> **Est-ce que chose vient encore souper avec nous?**
> Is what's-his-name coming to dinner again?

> **Écoute chose!**
> Listen you! Listen buster!

See GARS

Chum *m,f* (inf.) (from Engl., same pron.) Friend, buddy, boyfriend, girlfriend.

> **Mon chum Alain.**
> My buddy Al.

> **Son nouveau chum.**
> Her new boyfriend.

See AMI,E

Citron *m* Lemon.

> **Ma dernière auto était tout un citron.**
> My last car was a real lemon.

Cliquer [klee-kay] (from Engl.) To click, to hit it off.

> **Ça a bien cliqué entre nous.**
> We really hit it off.

> **"J'aime mon prochain, j'aime mon public,**
>   **Tout ce que je veux c'est que ça clique..."**
> From a song by Québec singer Robert Charlebois

J'étais choqué quand j'ai vu ma note finale!
I was really steamed when I saw my final mark!

See Choqué,e

Clou *m* **Ça tombe comme des clous!** (lit. *it's falling like nails*) It's raining cats and dogs!

You're heading out to lunch with your Québécois clients. Nearing the front doorway you suddenly see torrential rains coming down outside. You cry out "*Ayoille, ça tombe comme des clous!*" Your clients laugh — they couldn't have said it better.

Club [klub] or [kloob] *m* (from Engl.) Nightclub, or bar à la québécoise — often intimate with a unique atmosphere and style.

> **Savez-vous quel club les étudiants de McGill fréquentent?**
> Do you know which nightclub the McGill students go to?

Cœur *m* **Avoir le cœur sur la main** (lit. *to have one's heart on one's hand*) To be very generous.

> **Henri a le cœur sur la main.**
> Henry is very, very generous.

Coin *m* (lit. *corner*) Place, area.

> **Claude vient du coin du Lac-Saint-Jean.**
> Claude comes from the Lac-Saint-Jean area.
>
> **Restes-tu dans le coin?**
> Do you live around here (in this area)?

See BOUT

Comme ça 1. (may repl. *alors*) So.

> **Comme ça, qu'est-ce que vous avez décidé?**
> So, what have you decided?

See FAIT QUE

Ça tombe comme des clous!
(*It's falling like nails*)
It's raining cats and dogs!

See Clou

2.   (may repl. *comme ci comme ça*) A bit, so so.

> **As-tu aimé le spectacle? — Oui, comme ça.**
> Did you enjoy the show? — Yes, a bit.

Comment? (lit. *how*) How's that? What did you say? See PARDON

Comment ça? (may repl. *pourquoi*) How's that, why, why not?

> **Je peux pas aller à Bromont avec vous. — Comment ça?**
> I can't go to Bromont with you. — Why not?

Commérage *m* Gossiping. See PLACOTAGE

Commère *f* Gossip (the person).

> **Il est la commère de la ville.**
> He's the town gossip.

Comprendre Je comprends! (lit. *I understand*) You can say that again! I know what you mean!

> **Les professeurs ici sont trop exigeants. — Je comprends!**
> The teachers here are too demanding. — You can say that again!

Often pronounced *j'comprends* [sh'kawñ-prawñ]

Correct,e Okay, right. An indispensable part of your French vocabulary.

> **C'est correct!**
> That's okay!

> **C'est pas correct de faire ça.**
> It's not right to do that.

> **Monsieur Lavallée est correct avec ses employés.**
> Mr. Lavallée treats his employees right.

> **C'est ben correct!** (inf.)
> That's A-okay! No problem!

Note: *c'est correct* is often pronounced *c'correct* [scor-ek]

See BEAU; O.K.

Cou'don [coo-dawñ] (short form of *écoute donc*) Listen, hey listen.

> **Cou'don, si on faisait un tour de calèche dans le Vieux-Montréal?**
> Hey listen, how about going for a carriage ride in Old Montréal?

Coup *m* Blow, shot.

Donner un coup To put some effort into it, to give it one's best shot.

> **Donne un coup Guy si tu veux gagner!**
> Give it your best shot Guy if you want to win!

Manquer son coup To blow it.

> **As-tu peur de manquer ton coup?**
> Are you afraid of blowing it?

Prendre un coup To have a drink, to drink. (booze)

> **Viens prendre un coup après le travail!**
> Come on out for a drink after work!

> **Son père prend un coup.**
> His father drinks.

Couper les cheveux en quatre (lit. *to split hairs in four*) To split hairs.

> **Là, vous coupez les cheveux en quatre!**
> There, you're splitting hairs!

Course *f* Race **Être à la course** To race around, to be in a rush.

> **Les gens d'aujourd'hui sont toujours à la course.**
> People today are always in a rush.

Couru T'as couru après! (lit. *you ran after it*) You asked for it!

Crampant,e (lit. *cramping* or that which gives you cramps) Hilarious, a scream.

> **Il est crampant, ce comique-là!**
> That comedian is a scream!

C'tait [stay] (short form of *c'était*) It was.

> **C'tait ma fête hier.**
> It was my birthday yesterday.

Il est crampant, ce comique-là!
That comedian is a scream!

See Crampant

C't'un [stuñ] (short form of *c'est un*) It's a, he's a.

> **C't'un homme mystérieux.**
> He's a mysterious man.

C't'une [stoon] (short form of *c'est une*) It's a, she's a.

> **C't'une histoire incroyable!**
> That's an incredible story!

Culottes *f* Pants **Se faire déculotter** (lit. *to lose one's pants*) To lose all one's money.

> **Ces investisseurs vont se faire déculotter!**
> Those investors are going to lose everything!

See PERDRE SA CHEMISE

Curieux,-se Curious, nosy.

> **T'es assez curieuse!**
> You're pretty nosy, aren't you!

D

Débordé,e de travail (lit. *overflowing with work*) Swamped with work.

> **Depuis les mises à pied, je suis débordé de travail.**
> Since the lay-offs, I've been swamped with work.

Déjeuner, Dîner, Souper *m* (nouns or verbs) Breakfast, Lunch, Dinner.

From old 17th-century French, these words have carried on the tradition in Québec to remain the standard terms for meals. France's present-day equivalents are *petit déjeuner, déjeuner* and *dîner*.

> **On déjeune tôt chez nous.**
> We have early breakfasts at our place.

> **Monsieur Leblanc est parti dîner.**
> Mr. Leblanc has gone to lunch.

> **Le souper sera servi à six heures.**
> Dinner will be served at six.

Note that because of the strong influence of Parisian French, the Parisian equivalents may appear in written material and on some restaurant menus in Québec, causing confusion if not indigestion for the unprepared. But you won't be fooled!

Déniaise-toi! (inf.) Smarten up! Clean up your act! See NIAISER

Dépanneur *m* (from the verb *dépanner* — to help out, to tide over). A very fitting term for the corner or convenience stores found in most residential neighbourhoods.

> **Je vais au dépanneur chercher du vin blanc.**
> I'm going to the corner store for some white wine.

Diable *m* Devil.

> **Au diable** (lit. *to the devil with*) To heck with.
>
> > **Au diable le travail!**
> > To heck with the work!
>
> **Ça vaut pas le diable!** (lit. *it's not worth the devil*) It's worthless!
>
> **C'est pas un mauvais diable** (lit. *he's not a bad devil*) He's not a bad guy.

Difficile Difficult, fussy.

> **Jean-François mange pas dans n'importe quel restaurant, il est très difficile!**
> Jean-François doesn't eat in just any restaurant, he is very, very fussy!

Dîner See DÉJEUNER

Dîner d'affaires *m* Business lunch, businessmen's luncheon.

Dépanneur
Convenience store

Dire Je te l'avais dit! I told you so!

Dire quelque chose (lit. *to say something*) To ring a bell, to seem familiar.

> **Ton visage me dit quelque chose.**
> Your face rings a bell. Don't I know you from somewhere?

Dispendieux,-se (may repl. *cher*) Expensive.

> **Oui c'est beau, mais c'est bien trop dispendieux!**
> Yes it's beautiful, but it's far too expensive!

Dodo *m* (Kiddie talk) Beddy bye, sleep.

> **C'est le temps de faire dodo!**
> Time for beddy bye!

Doit Ça doit! It must be! It should be!

> **C'est-tu le vieux Albert? — Ça doit!**
> Is that old Albert? — Must be!

See TU

Drette [dret] *f* ** (var. of *droite*) Right.

> **Tu tournes à drette, pis tu tournes à gauche.**
> You turn right, then you turn left.

C'est-tu le vieux Albert? — Ça doit!
Is that old Albert? — Must be!

See Doit

Dur,e Hard **Faire dur** (inf.) 1. To look awful, to be homely.

> **Les Red Wings font dur ce soir.**
> The Red Wings look awful tonight. (their playing)

> **Ton petit chien fait dur.**
> That little dog of yours is pretty homely.

2. To be dumb, stupid.

> **Ça fait dur, déranger le monde comme ça.**
> It's dumb to bother people like that.

Dz See ZZZZZ

E

Écœurant,e (from *cœur* — heart) (inf.) awful, gross; great.

See SUPER

Écœurer (inf.) to turn off, to really annoy.

> **Ça m'écœure!**
> That's gross!

> **Le patron m'écœure.**
> The boss really annoys me.

Embarquer (lit. *to embark*) (inf.) 1. To interest, to attract.

> **Julie m'embarque**.
> Julie attracts me.

2. To take part in, to get involved.

> **J'embarque!**
> Count me in!

Embêtant,e Troublesome, annoying, puzzling.

> **Elles sont-tu embêtantes, ces grosses factures de téléphone!**
> Are these big phone bills a nuisance or whaaat!

Embêter To annoy, to worry, to puzzle.

> **Ça m'embête!**
> Beats me!

Énerver (from *nerf* — nerve) To get on someone's nerves.

> **Ce client m'énerve.**
> This customer gets on my nerves.

S'énerver To get angry, to lose one's cool.

> **Énerve-toi pas!**
> Take it easy!

Entendre S'entendre To get along well with people.

> **On s'entend très très bien!**
> We get along great!

Épouvantable Awful. See SUPER

Eux autres (lit. *those others*) (inf.) (may repl. *eux*) Them, those guys.

See VOUS AUTRES

Exagérer As in English, means *to exaggerate*, but can also mean *to go too far* or *to get carried away*.

Arrête d'exagérer Bertrand! Laisse-nous parler un peu.
Don't get so carried away Bert! Let the rest of us get a few words in edgewise.

Excuse, excusez Excuse me. Interchangeable with *pardon*, though most often used in Québec as an apology when someone must move or has been bumped.

See PARDON

Excusez!
Excuse me!

See Excuse

F

Faire à manger (may repl. *faire la cuisine*) To cook, to prepare a meal.

> **C'est qui qui va faire à manger ce soir?**
> Who's making dinner tonight?

Faire de bon Qu'est-ce que tu fais de bon? (lit. *what are you doing that's good*) What have you been up to lately? What's up?

> **Salut Alexandre! Qu'est-ce que tu fais de bon?**
> Hi Alex! What's up?

Faire du bien To do good. A general comment said about any state or action that produces a positive effect, be it pleasure or progress.

> **Un bon sauna chaud te fera du bien!**
> A nice hot sauna will do you good!

> **Merci pour avoir fait le ménage, ça fait du bien.**
> Thanks for tidying up, it really helps.

Fait que or **Ça fait que** (may repl. *alors*) So.

> **J'ai mon samedi de libre, fait qu'on peut aller dans la Beauce.**
> I'm free on Saturday, so we can go to Beauce county.

> **Ça fait que je te verrai samedi!**
> So, I'll see you Saturday!

See PIS

Farce *f* (may repl. *blague*) Joke, trick.

   Farce platte *f* (inf.) (lit. *flat joke*) Corny, dull joke, dirty trick.

   Est-ce que c'est lui qui raconte des farces plattes?
   Is he the one who tells the corny jokes?

   Charles m'a fait une farce platte.
   Charly played a dirty trick on me.

 C'est juste des farces! I'm just kidding!

Faut Il faut le faire! (lit. *it must be done*) That takes some doing!
That's really something!

   Il a frappé cinq circuits dans un seul match! — Il faut le faire!
   He hit five homers in just one game! — Hey, that takes some doing!

Feeling *m* (inf.) (from Engl., same pron.) (may repl. *sentiment*) Feeling.

   "C'est une question de feeling...oh, oh, oh ..."
   From a song by Québec singers Richard Cocciante and Fabienne Thibeault

See FILER

Fête *f* (from old French, usually repl. *anniversaire*) Birthday.

   Bonne fête Nicole!
   Happy birthday Nicole!

Fête _f_ **Chanson de fête** Birthday song.

There are not just one, but two common birthday songs in Québec. And if you wish to participate fully when the birthdays of Québécois friends and associates are celebrated, you should know both songs as either may be sung.

The traditional song is:

> _Bon-ne fête André,_
> _Bon-ne fête André,_
> _Bon-ne fête, bon-ne fête,_
> _Bon-ne fête André!_

Which is none other than Happy Birthday in French with minor variations in the lyrics. The proper name, of course, changes to suit the honoree.

In recent years, however, a second tune has been adopted by a great many Québécois as a birthday song. It all started back in the summer of 1975 when Gilles Vigneault (See CHANSONNIER) sang his _Gens du pays_ for the first time at that year's Saint-Jean-Baptiste Day celebration atop Mount Royal in Montréal. The song was an instant success, and its brief chorus soon caught on as something to be sung at birthdays.

Adapted, it goes:

> _Ma chère (Joanne)!_   (_Mon cher_ for men)
> _C'est à ton tour,_
> _De te laisser_
> _Parler d'amour._   (repeat all four lines)

The lyrics state that it is the birthday person's turn to be talked to about love.

On other occasions, you may find yourself singing this second tune to honour people's achievements, like a kind of "He's a jolly good fellow," or around the traditional June 24th bonfire to help celebrate Québec anniversaries.

Fête du travail *f* Labour Day.

Fête des mères *f* Mother's Day.

Fêter To celebrate, to live it up, to party.

> **On va fêter au Château Frontenac.**
> We're going to celebrate at the Château Frontenac.
>
> .

Fêtes *m* Christmas holiday, Christmas time.

> **Restez-vous à Montréal pendant les Fêtes? — Non, on va passer Noël avec ma famille en Abitibi.**
> Are you staying in Montréal at Christmas time? — No, we're going to spend Christmas with my family in Abitibi.

Filer [feel-ay] (inf.) (meaning taken from Engl. *feel*, may replace *se sentir*) To feel.

> **Je file pas**.
> I feel lousy.

See FEELING

Fin,e (lit. *fine*) Smart, (really) nice.

> **Danielle est assez fine pour réussir.**
> Daniela is smart enough to succeed.
>
> **Ton nouvel ami est fin!**
> Your new boyfriend is really nice!

Ma chère Joanne!
C'est à ton tour,
De te laisser
Parler d'amour.

See Fête, Chanson de

Flair *m* Intuition, a sense of things to come.

> **Il a du flair en affaires.**
> He has good business intuition.

Flasher [flash-ay] (from Engl.) (inf.) To be flashy, to be dressed flashy, to stand out.

> **Sylvie a flashé pas mal à la disco hier soir.**
> Sylvia was dressed really flashy at the disco last night.

Flyé,e [flī-ay] (inf.) A bit crazy, eccentric and/or weird.

> **Paul est flyé.**
> Paul's a real nutcake.

> **Ah non, la flyée est revenue!**
> Oh no, the crazy lady's back!

Fois *f* **Une bonne fois** (lit. *one good time*) Sometime, when possible.

> **Appelle-moi une bonne fois!**
> Call me sometime!

Foncer To do one's utmost, to go the extra mile.

> **Carole fonce dans son travail.**
> Carol goes the extra mile in her work.

Fonceur,-se Said of one who is ambitious, goes the extra mile, takes risks and achieves.

>**C'est un homme d'affaires fonceur.**
>He's a very gutsy businessman.

Forme *f* **Être en forme** (lit. *to be in shape*) To feel good, to be well.

>**Je suis en forme!**
>I feel good!
>
>**En forme, Stéphane?**
>How are you doing Steve?

Fou comme un balai (lit. *crazy like a broom*) Ecstatic, happy as a lark over something.

>**Papa est fou comme un balai avec sa nouvelle auto!**
>Dad's as happy as a lark with his new car!

Fou rire *m* (lit. *crazy laugh*) 1. A powerful, almost uncontrollable urge to laugh out loud in situations where such behaviour is taboo, e.g., in class, at public libraries, during the boss's monologue and so on. 2. The laughter itself when it erupts.

>**J'avais le fou rire!**
>I was just busting to laugh! *or*
>I couldn't stop laughing!

Here again the context indicates which meaning applies.

Foudre Coup de foudre *m* (lit. *bolt of lightning*) Love at first sight.

> **Ça a été le coup de foudre!**
> It was love at first sight!

Foutre S'en foutre or **S'en fouter** To not care at all.

> **Je m'en fous!**
> I couldn't care less!

Français,e *m,f* A French-speaking person. Among French Québecers, however, *un Français* is often a Frenchman from France and *une Française* a Frenchwoman.

> **C'est une Française.**
> She's a Frenchwoman (from France).

Français,e de France *m,f* Specifically, a Frenchman or Frenchwoman from France.

> **C'est un Français de France.**
> He's a Frenchman (from France).

See QUÉBÉCOIS

Franchement! (lit. *frankly*) Really! (in disapproval).

> **Franchement Lucie, tu critiques trop!**
> Really, Lucy, you criticize too much!

Coup de foudre
(*Bolt of lightning*)
Love at first sight

See Foudre

Frette [fret] ** (may repl. *froid*) Cold.

> **Il faisait frette à Chicoutimi.**
> It was cold in Chicoutimi.

Frileux,-se Said of one who is sensitive to the cold, and given Québec winters, which compare with the best this country can dish out, it's no wonder the word is so often heard.

> **Anne-Marie aime pas l'hiver, elle est trop frileuse.**
> Anne-Marie doesn't like winter, she gets cold too easily.

> **T'es frileux hein!**
> Can't take the cold eh!

Fumer comme une cheminée To smoke like a chimney.

> **Mon oncle fume comme une cheminée.**
> My uncle smokes like a chimney.

Fun *m* (inf.) (from Engl., same pron.) Everything is "*le fun*", it seems, in good old Québec, judging from the popularity of this English borrowing. To be sure, our francophone neighbours use the word carte blanche, to include everyday things that English speakers depict as *great* or *nice*, etc., rather than *fun*. Moreover, other French modifiers like *amusant, divertissant* and *plaisant* may be ousted to make way for *le fun* when speaking off the cuff at informal times.

> **Le ski alpin, c'est bien le fun!**
> Downhill skiing is a lot of fun!

> **C'est un livre le fun.**
> It's an entertaining book.

C'est le fun, cette émission-là.
That show's great!

C'est le fun d'aller au parc Mont-Royal.
Mount Royal Park is a nice place to go.

C'est le fun ce que tu dis là.
What you're saying is very interesting.

May also be spelled: *fonne*.

Le ski alpin, c'est bien le fun!
Downhill skiing is a lot of fun!

See Fun

G

Gars *m* Guy.

Connais-tu ce gars-là?
Do you know that guy?

Bon gars Good guy.

Simon est un bon gars.
Simon's a good guy.

Mon gars Sonny boy, kiddo.

Écoute, mon gars!
Listen kiddo!

Gêné,e Sois pas gêné (lit. *don't be shy*) Feel free, don't hesitate.

Appelle-moi quand tu voudras, sois pas gêné.
Call whenever you want, just feel free.

T'es pas gêné?! (lit. *aren't you embarrassed?*) You've got a lot of nerve! You should be ashamed of yourself!

T'es pas gêné Maxime?! On demande pas ça la première fois qu'on sort ensemble!
You've got a lot of nerve Max asking me that on our first date!

Gêner Gêne-toi pas! Go right ahead! Feel free!

Gêne-toi pas, fais comme chez toi!
Go right ahead and make yourself at home!

Gourmand,e *m,f* One who over-indulges at the table or snacks too much, regardless of whether that person qualifies as a *gourmet*.

T'es gourmand!
You eat too much!

Goût *m* Taste **Avoir le goût** (may repl. *avoir envie*) To feel like.

Denise a le goût de danser.
Denise feels like dancing.

See TENTER

Grand-chose *m* **Pas grand-chose** Not much, not a whole lot.

Qu'est-ce que tu fais ce soir Chantal? — Pas grand-chose!
What are you doing tonight Chantal? — Not a whole lot!

Granola *m,f* A woman who eats mostly health foods, wears simple dress — including lots of wool — and has a very natural life style. Also said of men.

C'est une granola.
She's a health food nut.

C'est un granola.
He's earthy.

T'es granola!
You're such a·hippie!

Granola

Grave (lit. *serious*) Terrible, a real case. A comment made about those who appear to be extreme in their behaviour or attitudes.

> **La femme qui travaille là est vraiment grave. — Oui, elle est toujours impolie.**
> The lady working there is really terrible. — Yes, she's always rude.

C'est pas grave! It's no big deal! It doesn't matter!

> **Écoute, Charles, c'est pas grave!**
> Listen Charly, it's no big deal!

Grignoter To snack.

> **Lise adore grignoter.**
> Lisa loves to snack.

Grimper dans les rideaux (lit. *to climb in the curtains*) What our francophone friends do in their moments of frustration while we're busy climbing the wall.

> **O.K., arrête, grimpe pas dans les rideaux!**
> Hold on now, don't climb the wall!

Grosse légume *f* (lit. *big vegetable*) Big shot.

> **C'est les grosses légumes de la compagnie!**
> They're the company big shots!

Grimper dans les rideaux
(*To climb in the curtains*)
To climb the wall

H

Habillé,e comme la chienne à Jacques (lit. *dressed like Jack's dog*) Dressed loudly, or in a sloppy manner.

Here's a bitingly pertinent remark that can be made about that friend of yours who doesn't give two hoots for style.

> **Il est habillé comme la chienne à Jacques!**
> What a slob!

Habiller Bien s'habiller To get dressed up.

> **On doit bien s'habiller pour ce party.**
> We have to get dressed up for this party.

> **S'habiller chic** To dress with flair, to dress trendy.

> **Tu t'habilles chic aujourd'hui Frédéric!**
> You're looking pretty trendy today Fred!

See CHIC; TENUE

Haïr To hate **J'haïs pas ça!** (lit. *I don't hate it*) I don't mind!

Note: *haïs* [ī-ee] is the Québec pronunciation.

Haïssable [ī-ee-sabl] or [ī-ee-sab] (lit. *hateable*) Rotten, nasty (often said tongue in cheek).

> **Pourquoi t'es si haïssable?**
> Why are you so rotten?

Hâte *f* Haste **Avoir hâte** To be anxious.

Note that the speaker may be referring to either a good or bad kind of anxiousness. Look at the context to determine which.

> **As-tu hâte de me voir? — Oui j'ai hâte!**
> Are you anxious to see me? — I sure am!

> **Gilles a hâte que la journée finisse.**
> Giles is anxious for the day to be over.

Heure *f* **À c't'heure** [a-ster] ** (short form of *à cette heure*) (may repl. *maintenant*) Now, at this moment.

> **Il fait soleil à c't'heure.**
> It's sunny out now.

You may see this also notated *asteur*.

Hein! Eh! Yes, our French friends say it too. It's the Québécois rendition of the famous Canadian "*eh*" with one slight twist. That is, once across the border just east of Cornwall or a little north of Edmundston (or a stone's throw east of Atwater Avenue in Montréal), you start rounding it off with a very gallic nasal sound.

> **Hein? Qu'est-ce que t'as dit?** [ayñ] **
> Eh? What did you say?

> **J'ai dit "vous parlez bien le français, hein!"** [uñ]
> I said "you speak French very well, eh!"

For added pomp and circumstance, some French speakers will let the nasal sound vibrate a little in their nostrils while ebbing it up to an airy finale. Here, the English "eh" doesn't cut it.

> **Je suis le maître d'hôtel heinnnnnnnn!**
> I'm the maître d' you know!

C'est les grosses légumes de la compagnie!
(*They're the company's big vegetables*)
They're the company big shots!

See Grosse légume

I

I [ee] See Y

Icitte [ee-sit] ** (var. of *ici*) Here.

> **Viens icitte!**
> Come here!

Idée *f* **Changer les idées** (lit. *to change one's ideas*) To provide a change, a change of scene, to get one's mind off something.

> **Une semaine à la campagne va me changer les idées.**
> A week in the country will give me a change of scene.

Instant *m* **Un instant!** Just a second!

> **Un instant s'il vous plaît!**
> Just a second please!

Usually more polite than *Minute!*

See MINUTE

J

Jaser To make conversation, chat, talk up a storm, etc. Evoking that long-noted Québécois predisposition for friendly conversation and spirited verbal expression.

>**Elle a jasé longtemps avec sa grande chum Sylvie.**
>She talked away the day with her close friend Sylvia.

Jos connaissant or **Jos connaisseur** *m* (lit. *knowing Joe*) Know-it-all.

>**Arrête de faire ton Jos connaissant!**
>Stop being such a know-it-all!

Note: *Jos* is pronounced like *Joe*.

Joie de vivre *f* Joy of living, zest for life.

>**Marc-André a de la joie de vivre.**
>Marc-André has a zest for life.

Joual [jwal] *m* (from an informal pron. of *cheval* — horse).

The term *joual* was coined by André Laurendeau of *Le Devoir* and given prominence by Jean-Paul Desbiens (pen name *Frère Untel*) in the early 1960s for what they saw as a deterioration in the quality of the French spoken in Québec. Since then, Québec society has undergone profound social and economic change, its culture has blossomed and the language has evolved. Throughout this period, the word *joual* has continued to be used to describe spoken French and has been attributed various meanings.

Pop star Robert Charlebois, for instance, is said to have broken with the past in 1970 by incorporating extensive *joual* into the lyrics of his songs. Charlebois was considered by many to be the voice of a new generation, and *joual* the symbol of a distinct Québécois language and culture. The plays of Michel Tremblay, created in the same era, are said also to be written in *joual*. Yet *joual* here is equated with the lingo of the urban working class and could be interpreted as signifying a wide range of informal language and slang. Other observers have associated *joual* with the speech of various rural areas of Québec.

Today, in general conversation, a Québécois colleague may tell you that a certain word is *joual* and that another would be more appropriate. In this case, *joual* means slang. Note that to denote slang typical of France, Québecers use the term *argot*.

Reference: Encyclopedia of Canada
             Les insolences du frère Untel
             La chanson québécoise

Jouer Va jouer dans le trafic! (lit. *go play in the traffic*) Go jump in the lake! Get Lost!

Journée *f* **C'est pas ma journée!** This just isn't my day!

J'sais [jsay] (short form of *je sais*) I know.

> **T'es en retard! — J'sais!**
> You're late! — I know!

98

J'suis [shwee] (short form of *je suis*) I'm.

> **J'suis de bonne humeur.**
> I'm in a good mood. I feel good.

K

Kick *m* (from Engl., same pron.) **Pour le kick!** (lit. *for the kick*) Just for kicks! Just for the fun of it!

Kit *m* (from Engl., same pron.) **Tout le kit** (lit. *the whole kit*) Everything, the whole bit.

> **Ils ont servi du champagne et tout le kit!**
> They served champagne and the whole bit!

L

L (consonant) Is sometimes dropped or not fully sounded in spoken Québec French. Examples:

The *l* in *la* (the) is dropped and the word is pronounced [a] **.

Je vais à la banque becomes *Je vais à 'a banque*, pronounced [juu vayz a bawñk] I'm going to the bank.

Les (plural of *the*) becomes *'es*, pronounced [ay] (inf.).

Hence, *tous les deux* becomes *tous 'es deux* [too ay duh] Both of them.

Lui (him, her) becomes *'ui*, pronounced [wee] or [ee] (inf.).

Je 'ui ai dit. [jee ay dzee]
I told him.

Il (he, it) becomes *I'*, pronounced [ee].

I' est montréalais.
He's a Montréaler.

See Y

Là [la] or [law] (lit. *there*) May be added for emphasis or as a style of speech.

Minute, là!
Just a minute!

Qu'est-ce qui va pas, là?
What's the matter?

J'ai mis tes clefs là, là.
I put your keys there.

Lâche pas! (lit. *don't let go*) Hang in there! Go for it!

Lâche pas, Édouard, t'es capable!
Hang in there Ed, you can do it!

See VAS-Y

Laisse faire! Never mind! Forget it!

Laisse faire, Grégoire! Je vais le faire moi-même.
Never mind Greg! I'll do it myself.

Là Là [la law] (lit. *there there*) (inf.) 1. There, over there somewhere.

2. Well, as far as that's concerned....

Langue *f* **Ne pas avoir la langue dans sa poche** (lit. *to not have one's tongue in one's pocket*) Said of people in relation to their verbosity to indicate that they either talk a lot, are not afraid to speak their mind or have the gift of the gab.

Il a pas la langue dans sa poche, il serait super en politique!
He's got the gift of the gab, he'd be great in politics!

See BAVARD

101

Il a pas la langue dans sa poche!
(*He doesn't have his tongue in his pocket*)
He's got the gift of the gab!

See Langue

Laver (lit. *to wash*) To clobber, to cream.

> **Les Expos ont lavé les Dodgers hier soir.**
> The Expos creamed the Dodgers last night.

Lui-même! (lit. *himself*) (on phone, may repl. *c'est moi*) Speaking!

> **Puis-je parler à Monsieur Gagnon? — Lui-même!**
> May I speak to Mr. Gagnon? — Speaking!

Loup *m* **Avoir une faim de loup** (lit. *to have a wolf's hunger*) To be famished, to have a big appetite.

> **J'ai une faim de loup!**
> I'm ravenous!

Lune *f* **Être dans la lune** (lit. *to be in the moon*) To be in the clouds, to daydream.

> **Mes élèves sont dans la lune aujourd'hui.**
> My students are in the clouds today.

Avoir une faim de loup
(*To have a wolf's hunger*)
To be famished, to have a big appetite

See Loup

M

Mâcher **Ne pas mâcher ses mots** (lit. *to not chew one's words*) To not mince words, to be blunt.

>**Ce gars-là mâche pas ses mots!**
>That guy doesn't mince words!

Madame, Mademoiselle, Monsieur Madam, Miss, Sir.

Part of the fun of speaking French in Québec is calling everyone in public either "*Madame*", "*Mademoiselle*" or "*Monsieur*" — something we don't find to nearly the same extent in everyday Canadian and American English. And *vive la différence!* For it offers an interesting change from the usual and familiar. Be aware too that there's nothing terribly formal about it: all French Québecers commonly employ these terms when speaking to people they don't know personally.

For anglophones venturing out into French-speaking circles, the challenge is to use the terms correctly. While perfection is not *de rigueur*, it is satisfying to know we are speaking French the way the French do. You, the reader, shall excel in this pursuit. With the following pointers, you will be completely ready to get out there and hobknob!

- Technically, *Madame* is the proper term for a married woman.

- In practice, usage tends to follow age, older women being addressed as *Madame*, younger women as *Mademoiselle.*

- *Madame* applies when you have no idea of a woman's marital status or age (when talking on the phone, for example), and, in this instance, it corresponds to the English *Ms.*

- Very young women (teenagers and rising) are always called *Mademoiselle*. Don't worry, however, should you happen to get it wrong — a young Québécoise will straighten you out immediately, since to her, *Madame* sounds as old as the hills!

- For gents, life is simpler — the one term *Monsieur* covers men of all ages.

> **Bonjour Madame!**
> Hello! (Madam)
>
> **Merci Mademoiselle!**
> Thank you! (Miss)
>
> **S'il vous plaît, Monsieur!**
> Please! (Sir)

See VOUS vs. TU

Magané,e [ma-ga-nay] (inf.) Wrecked, busted, worn out.

Here we're looking at a life-saver that's always there when you need one quick word to cover the whole gamut of things that can deteriorate. Because it will allow you to describe *run down* cars (usé), *run down* people (épuisé), *ruined* material (abîmé), *broken* or *damaged* objects (brisé, endommagé), *spoiled* goods (abîmé) and machines *on the blink* (hors d'usage).

The words in brackets are from standard Québec French and are naturally available when you wish to be more specific or formal in your speech.

> **Mes jeans sont maganés.**
> My jeans are worn out.
>
> **La télévision est maganée!**
> The TV's busted!

Maganer [ma-ga-nay] (inf.) (may repl. *briser*) To wreck, to bust.

> **Magane pas mon auto!**
> Don't wreck my car!

Magasiner (from *magasin* — store) To shop, to go shopping.

> **Elle adore magasiner sur la rue Sainte-Catherine.**
> She loves shopping on St. Catherine Street.

Manche *f* Une autre paire de manches (lit. *another pair of sleeves*) Another kettle of fish.

> **Ça, Claude, c'est une autre paire de manches!**
> That, Claude, is another kettle of fish!

Manquer le bateau To miss the boat.

> **T'as manqué le bateau Robert, la fille de tes rêves vient juste de se marier!**
> You missed the boat Rob, the girl of your dreams has just gotten married!

Masse *f* En masse (inf.) Loads, tons.

> **Olivier a de l'argent en masse.**
> Oliver's got loads of money.

Meilleur,e (lit. *best*) (may repl. *préféré*) Favourite.

> **Daniel Lavoie est mon meilleur chanteur.**
> Daniel Lavoie is my favourite singer.

Mêlant [mel-awñ] Confusing, tricky.

> **C'est mêlant.**
> It's confusing.

C'est pas mêlant! It's as simple as that! It's a fact!

> **Vous allez réussir, c'est pas mêlant!**
> You're going to succeed, it's as simple as that!

Mêlé,e Mixed up, lost.

> **Je suis tout mêlé.**
> I'm all mixed up.

Merci Mille fois merci! A thousand thanks!

Merci quand même! or **Merci pareil!** Thanks anyway!

Moé [mwoy] ** (var. of *moi*) Me.

> **Lui pis moé.**
> Him and me.

See TOÉ

Minute! Just a minute!

> **Minute! J'ai pas fini.**
> Just a minute! I haven't finished.

See INSTANT

Mon vieux! (lit. *my old one*) Old buddy!

> **Comment ça va mon vieux?**
> How's it going old buddy?

Monsieur See MADAME, MADEMOISELLE

Moral *m* **Avoir le moral à terre** (lit. *to have one's morale on the ground*) To be down in the dumps, to have low morale.

> **Le pauvre Éric a le moral à terre.**
> Poor Eric is down in the dumps.

Mouiller (inf.) (may repl. *pleuvoir*) To rain.

> **Apporte ton parapluie, il mouille.**
> Bring your umbrella, it's raining.

Mouton *m* **Revenons à nos moutons** (lit. *let's get back to our sheep*) Let's get back to the point.

> **Bon, messieurs, revenons à nos moutons.**
> Now, gentlemen, let's get back to the point.

N

Ne is required in written French to form negative structures, such as *je ne sais pas — I do not know*. It's dropped, however, in most spoken French, being generally considered an unnecessary extra.

French speakers, in fact, are either unaware that they drop their *ne*s or perceive them as too formal sounding and more suited to writing. Hence, *pas* often stands alone to signal negation and is the key word to listen for in ascertaining all the nos, can'ts, couldn'ts and wouldn'ts of everyday life.

In typical conversation, our example *je ne sais pas* becomes *je sais pas* or, with the cat away, the words may play together to form *j'sais pas* [jsay paw].

Other words often jilted to negate on their own are *rien* (nothing), *aucun* (none) and *plus* (no more). They do the job nicely, though, and the aloof *ne* is hardly missed.

All in all, one finds that the music of the language changes when moving out of the classroom into the real world of spoken French where *ne* seldom intervenes and there's a whole new set of sounds blending into sounds to recognize.

Niaiser [nee-e-zay] (inf.) To fool around, to kid.

> **Arrête donc de niaiser!**
> Stop fooling around!
>
> **Je te niaise, voyons!**
> I'm just kidding you!

See DÉNIAISE-TOI

Niaiseux,-se *m,f* [nee-e-zuh, -uhz] (inf.) Dumb, turkey, nerd.

>**C'est niaiseux!**
>That's dumb!

>**C'est un gros niaiseux!**
>He's a real turkey!

Nous autres (lit. *us others*) (inf.) (may repl. *nous*) Us, us guys.

>**Viens-tu avec nous autres au Mont Tremblant?**
>Are you coming with us guys to Mount Tremblant?

See VOUS AUTRES

Nuit *f* **Passer la nuit sur la corde à linge** (lit. *to spend the night on the clothesline*) Calling all insomniacs! Here's a good expression for you. It means that you, poor wretches, had another one of those loooooong sleepless nights.

>**Pourquoi tu bailles comme ça Lucien? — Parce que j'ai passé la nuit sur la corde à linge!**
>Why are you yawning like that, Lucien? — Because I was up all night — couldn't sleep!

Passer la nuit sur la corde à linge
(*To spend the night on the clothesline*)
To have a sleepless night

See Nuit

O

O Canada!

Have you ever wondered how our bilingual national anthem sounds in Québec or exactly what the official French version says?

Well, beyond your wild enthusiasm or mere curiosity, knowing this could be extremely useful on outings to some hallowed Québec institutions, as the following scenario depicts.

...Wow! You're in the Montréal Forum. It's Hockey Night in Canada and the game's about to begin. But first the "National Anthem"! Yes, you rise ceremoniously to its long, majestic call, beaming with pride and ready to sing your heart out, when, suddenly, the French verse rings forth! Well you'd like to belt it out, by George, but haven't got a clue where to begin. And ain't it a pity!!...

So to make this unknown territory a little more familiar and help you commit it to memory, here it is in print, accompanied all the way by an unofficial English translation:

O Canada!
O Canada!

Terre de nos aïeux,
Land of our forbears,

Ton front est ceint de fleurons glorieux!   (like "glorious
Your head is crowned with flowers of glory!   and free")

Car ton bras sait porter l'épée,   ("we stand on
For your arm can bear the sword,   guard")

113

Il sait porter la croix!
It can bear the cross!

("we are a spiritual
people")

Ton histoire est une épopée,
Your history is an epic,

Des plus brillants exploits,
Of the most brilliant exploits,

Et ta valeur,
Your valour,

De foi trempée,
Soaked in faith,

Protégera nos foyers et nos droits,
Will protect our homes and our rights,

Protégera nos foyers et nos droits.
Will protect our homes and our rights.

That's how O Canada, our *hymne national*, sounds in Québec. And the next time Hockey Night in Canada or any other national event rolls into *la belle province*, you'll not only be prepared to sing along, but you'll have an intimate, insider's understanding of what it's all about.

Oeil *m* **Mon œil!** (lit. *my eye*) My Foot! It's not true!

Oeuf *m* **Mettre tous ses œufs dans le même panier** To put all one's eggs in one basket.

Officiel **C'est officiel!** (lit. *it's official*) That's for sure! That's a fact!

Often pronounced *c't'officiel* [stow-fee-syel]

114

See Oeil

O.K.! (from Engl., same pron.) 1. (may repl. *d'accord*) Okay! (consent).

2. Right, un hun, I see. Stated by the listener in a conversation as a sign of attention or understanding. Now, as a good listener, you may also wish to interject *Ah oui?* (Oh yeah?), *C'est vrai?* (Really?), *Bon!* (Good), *C'est bien!* (That's good).

O.K. d'abord! Okay then! Okeydoke!

On One, they, we. Most often used to mean *we* in daily speech, replacing *nous* as the sentence subject, and is quicker and more natural than some structures with *nous*.

Compare *on s'est vu* with *nous nous sommes vus*. Both mean "we saw each other", yet the shorter *on s'est vu* is almost always preferred.

Ouais! [way] or [wī] Yeah! Yep!

Ouache! [wa-sh] Yuk!

Ouf! [oof] or [uuf] 1. Phew!

> **Ouf! Ça a passé proche!**
> Phew! That was a close call!

2. Well, I don't know ...(combined with the famous Trudeau shrug).

> **Ouf...c'est possible que vous ayez tort.**
> Well, I don't know...you could be wrong.

Variations: *Wouf!*, *Bouf!*

Ouf!
Well, I don't know about that....

Ouvrage *m* (may repl. *travail*) Work.

Excuse-moi, mais j'ai de l'ouvrage à faire.
Excuse me, but I have work to do.

P

Paix *f* **La paix!** (lit. *the peace*) Leave me alone! Be quiet!

Paniquer (lit. *to panic*) (inf.) To worry, to be nervous.

> **Arrête de paniquer Benoît, l'examen va être facile.**
> Stop worrying Benoît, the exam's going to be easy.

See ÉNERVER

Pantoute [pawñ-tuut] (inf.) (may repl. *pas du tout*) Not at all, none at all.

> **J'aime pas pantoute cette boisson.**
> I don't like this drink at all.

> **Y en a-t-il? — Pantoute!**
> Are there any? — None at all!

Papier *m* **Je t'en passe un papier!** (lit. *I'm passing you a piece of paper*) I guarantee it! Take my word for it!

Paquet de (inf.) Whole bunch, bundle.

> **Je suis un paquet de nerfs.**
> I'm a bundle of nerves.

> **Elle a acheté un paquet d'affaires.**
> She bought a whole bunch of things.

Pardon? Pardon me?

> **Pardon? Répétez s'il vous plaît.**
> Pardon me? Could you repeat that please?
>
> See COMMENT; EXCUSE

Par exemple (lit. *for example*) 1. However, mind you.

> **Elle reste à Montréal, mais elle vient d'Halifax, par exemple.**
> She lives in Montréal... she comes from Halifax, mind you.

2. (inf.) Said for emphasis, or as a style of speech.

> **C'est gentil, par exemple!**
> That's pretty darn nice!

Parfait! (lit. *perfect*) Fine!

Heard frequently in business circles.

> **Parfait, Monsieur Leblanc, je vais donner votre message à Madame Gagnon. — C'est parfait!**
> Fine Mr. Leblanc, I'll give your message to Mrs. Gagnon. — That's fine!

Parlable (inf.) (lit. *talkable*) In a talking mood, approachable **Pas parlable** Untalkative, unapproachable.

> **T'es pas parlable ce matin!**
> I can't even speak to you this morning you're so grouchy!

120

Parler Là tu parles! (lit. *there you're talking*) Now you're talking!

> **Qu'est-ce que tu dirais d'un bon vin français? — Là tu parles!**
> What would you say to a good French wine? — Now you're talking!

Paroisse *f* Parish (sometimes, but not always!)

In conversation with francophone Québecers, the word *paroisse* is bound to pop up sooner or later. And while it reflects the imposing presence of the Catholic Church in Québec society up to the late 1950s, it may be heard in a general sense with no reference to the cloth. Because the *paroisse* in Québec has always been "a subdivision of a county, which functions both as an ecclesiastical and political unit."* And Québecers will often say it, not in connection with their parish, but simply to name the district or rural municipality in which they live.

> **Véronique reste dans la même paroisse que moi.**
> Veronica lives in the same district as me.

* Dictionary of Canadianisms

Party [par-tay] *m* or *f* (from Engl., may repl. *soirée*) Party.

> **Le party d'Halloween était super!**
> The Halloween party was great!

Pas mal (may repl. *très*) Very, really.

> **Les joueurs sont pas mal fatigués.**
> The players are very tired.

121

PAROISSE
PARISH

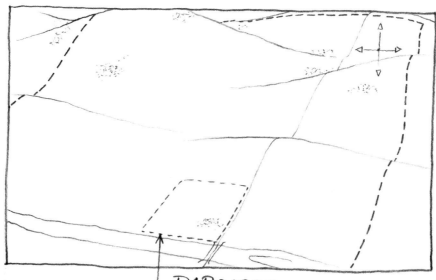

PAROISSE
DISTRICT, SUBDIVISION OF A COUNTY

Pas mal de (may repl. *beaucoup*) A lot.

> **Maurice a pas mal de contacts d'affaires.**
> Morris has a lot of business contacts.

Pas plus que ça Not that much, that's all?

> **Ton père, aime-t-il la pêche? — Pas plus que ça.**
> Does your father like fishing? — Not that much.

> **J'ai aimé le spectacle un peu. — Pas plus que ça?**
> I liked the show a bit. — That's all?

Passer (may repl. *prêter*) To lend.

> **Passe-moi cinq dollars, hein?**
> Lend me five dollars, will you?

Passer chez, à To drop in, to come by.

> **Nous sommes passés chez Georges.**
> We dropped in at George's.

> **Passez à mon bureau à deux heures.**
> Come by my office at two o'clock.

Patates *f* Potatoes **Être dans les patates** (lit. *to be in the potatoes*) To be totally wrong, to be way out in left field.

> **Ton comptable est dans les patates avec ces calculs.**
> Your accountant is way out in left field on these calculations.

Ton comptable est dans les patates avec ces calculs!
(*Your accountant is in the potatoes with these calculations*)
Your accountant is way out in left field on these calculations!

See Patates

Patente *f* (lit. *patent*) (inf.) Darn thing, thing-a-ma-jig.

> **Cette patente-là, elle marche jamais!**
> That darn thing never works!

Perdre sa chemise To lose one's shirt, to lose all one's money.

> **Le pauvre Raymond a perdu sa chemise dans le krach de la bourse.**
> Poor Ray lost his shirt in the stock market crash.

As you can see, francophone entrepreneurs, like their anglophone associates, risk losing their shirts in the fickle world of finance. Our French-speaking partners, however, stand to risk even more....

See CULOTTES

Petit change *m* (inf.) Small change **Prendre tout son petit change** (lit. *to take all one's small change*) To take everything one has, all one's courage.

> **Ça m'a pris tout mon petit change pour te dire ça.**
> It took me everything I have to tell you that.

Peut Ça se peut! It could be! Maybe!

> **Vas-tu visiter tes amis sur la Côte-Nord cet été? — Ça se peut!**
> Are you going to visit your friends on the North Shore this summer? — Could be!

Piasse or **Piastre** [pyas] *f* (inf.) Buck. Historically, the *piastre* was a unit of Spanish currency that circulated in the colonies of North

America; in the 1800s, it became the official French term in Canada for *dollar*. The word somehow lost its lettres de noblesse in the 20th century to become an everyday fun term that French Québecers sometimes use in place of *dollar*.

> **Voici tes cinq piasses.**
> Here's your five bucks.

Reference: Dictionnaire du français plus

See ARGENT

Pied *m* **Comme un pied** (lit. *like a foot*) Like an idiot, stupidly.

> **Tu conduis comme un pied!**
> You drive like an idiot!

Pipe *f* **Mets ça dans ta pipe!** (lit. *put that in your pipe*) Put that in your pipe and smoke it! So there!

Piquant *m* Spice **Mettre du piquant** To add some spice.

> **Ça met du piquant dans la vie!**
> It adds a bit of spice to life!

Pire Pas pire (lit. *not worse*) (inf.) (may repl. *pas mal*) Not bad.

> **Les résultats sont pas pires.**
> The results aren't bad.

Tu conduis comme un pied!
(*You drive like a foot*)
You drive like an idiot!

See Pied

Pas pire pas pire! Not too darn bad! Not bad at all!
Listen carefully to how this is said to capture its resonant Québécois
inflection while putting some oomph into it!

Comment ça va Marc? — Pas pire pas pire!
How's it going Mark? — Not too darn bad!

Pis [peeh] (inf.) (short form of *puis*) Then, and, so.

Y a attendu, pis y est parti.
He waited, then he left.

Toé pis moé.
You and me.

Pis Jean, quoi de neuf?
So John, what's new?

Pis!
So what!

Placotage [pla-ku-taj] *m* (usually repl. *bavardage*) Gabbing, gossiping.

See COMMÉRAGE

Placoter [pla-ku-tay] (usually repl. *bavarder*) To gab, to gossip.

Arrête de placoter au téléphone!
Stop gabbing on the phone!

Platte [plat] (lit. *flat*) Boring, a drag.

> **Le film était platte.**
> The movie was boring.
>
> **C'est une situation bien platte!**
> This situation is really a drag!

Plein C'est en plein ça! (lit. *it's that in full*) That's exactly it! Right on!

> **C'est en plein ça, c'est le mot que je cherchais.**
> That's exactly it, that's the word I was looking for.
>
> **L'environnement, c'est l'affaire de tous.**
> **— C'est en plein ça!**
> The environment is everyone's concern.
> — Right on!

Usually pronounced: *c't'en plein ça* [stawñ-pleñ-sa].

Pluie *f* **Faire la pluie et le beau temps** (lit. *to make it rain and shine*) To run the show.

> **C'est lui qui fait la pluie et le beau temps dans cette compagnie.**
> He's the one who runs the show in this company.

Pogné,e [pun-yay] (inf.) 1. Hung up (emotionally).

> **Arthur est ben pogné.**
> Art is really hung up.

2.   (may repl. *pris, coincé*) Caught, stuck.

Son foulard était pogné dans la porte.
Her scarf was caught in the door.

Pogner [pun-yay] (inf.) 1. To be popular, a hit, successful.

Céline Dion pogne aux États-Unis!
Célinc Dion's a hit in the States!

2.   (may repl. *attraper*) To get, to catch.

J'ai pogné la grippe.
I caught a cold.

Poisson d'avril! *m* (lit. *April fish*) April fool's!

Pot *m* **Arrête de tourner autour du pot!** (lit. *stop turning around the pot*) Quit beating around the bush!

Prendre Se prendre pour un autre (lit. *to take oneself to be another*) To think quite highly of oneself.

Pour qui elle se prend?
Who does she think she is?

Prix *m* **Ne pas avoir de prix** (lit. *to have no price*) To be priceless, to be invaluable.

> **L'amitié a pas de prix, mon fils!**
> You can't put a price tag on friendship, my son!

P'tit [ptsee] The Québécois pronunciation of *petit* — *small*, and one of the rich tonal ingredients that give Québec French its own special sound. The feminine form is **P'tite** [ptseet].

See TI; TS

Pus [pew] (inf.) (short form of *plus*) No more, any more.

> **Il y en a pus.**
> There's no more.
>
> **J'y vais pus.**
> I don't go there any more.

See L

Q

Québécois,e *m,f* Québecer, or French-speaking Québecer as opposed to a Frenchman or Frenchwoman from France.

C'est un Québécois.
He's a Québecer.

Elle est québécoise, pas française.
She's a French Québecer, not a Frenchwoman.

See FRANÇAIS,E; FRANÇAIS,E DE FRANCE

Que c'est ça?! (inf.) What the heck is that?!

Qu'est-ce que ça donne? (lit. *what does it give*) What result does it produce? What good does it do?

Qu'est-ce que ça fait? (lit. *what does it do*) What difference does it make? What of it?

Qu'est-ce que tu as? (lit. *what do you have*) What's the matter? What's the matter with you?

Qu'est-ce qui te prend? (lit. *what's taking you*) What's got into you? What's your problem? Get real!

132

Que'que [kek] (inf.) (short form of *quelque*) Some.

> **Cherches-tu que'que chose?**
> Are you looking for something?

See L

Question *f* **Pas question!** No way!

> **Est-ce que je peux prendre ta nouvelle auto papa?**
> **— Pas question!**
> Can I borrow your new car Dad?
> — Noooo way!

Quoi De quoi (may repl. *quelque chose*) Something.

> **Je vais te dire de quoi!**
> I'll tell you something! Listen to this!

> **Ça m'a fait de quoi de la voir si triste.**
> It really did something to me to see her so sad.

Quoi de neuf? (lit. *what of new*) What's new?

> **Quoi de neuf Pierre?**
> What's new Pete?

Rat de bibliothèque
(*Library rat*)
Bookworm

R

Racké,e (inf.) (lit. *racked*) Worn out, dead beat.

> **Comment ça va, Richard? — Mal, je suis racké!**
> How's it going Richy? — Bad, I'm dead beat!

Rat de bibliothèque *m* (lit. *library rat*) Bookworm.

Rendez-vous *m* In English *rendezvous* means meeting at a designated place and time. In French it's that, plus the standard term for *date* and *appointment*.

> **Il a un rendez-vous avec Sophie ce soir. — Ayoille!**
> He has a date with Sophia tonight. — Wow!

> **Puis-je avoir un rendez-vous à 3h?**
> Can I make an appointment for 3 o'clock?

Revenir J'en reviens pas! (lit. *I don't come back from it*) I can't get over it! I don't believe it!

See VOYAGE

Rêver en couleur (lit. *to dream in colour*) To be really dreaming, to be really imagining things (nice things, that is).

> **Vous rêvez en couleur si vous pensez devenir riche comme ça.**
> You're really dreaming if you expect to get rich like that.

Rien Il y a rien là! (lit. *there's nothing there*) ** It's no big deal! No problem!

Usually pronounced *Y a rien là* [ee-ya ree-añ law]

See GRAVE; Y

See Revenir

S

Sac *m* **C'est dans le sac!** It's in the bag!

Sacre [sakruu] or [sak] *m* (usually repl. *juron*) Swearword.

As the term itself suggests, most of the principal swearwords heard in Québec are derived from the sacred items of the Church. Two excellent sources to consult on this subject are the *Handbook of Québec and Acadian French* and *Sacres et blasphèmes québécois* (see bibliography), which offer an impressively thorough review of this aspect of everyday language. The latter even delves into the psychology of swearing and the role it has played in Québec literature, film and theatre, as well as daily life.

> **Tabarnouche!** [ta-bar-noosh] and **Câline!** [caw-leen] are two common euphemisms for the real thing — *tabarnak* and *câlice*. The beauty of these euphemisms is that they are completely inoffensive and can be said in even the best of company.

Sacrer (usually repl. *jurer*) To swear.

> **Est-ce que tu sacres beaucoup?**
> Do you swear a lot?

Salut! Hi! *or* Bye!

Remember this common turn of phrase:

> **Bon ben, salut là!**
> Well, see you round then!

See ALLÔ; BONJOUR

138

Sapin *m* **Se faire passer un sapin** (lit. *to be handed a fir tree*) To get taken for a ride, to be had.

> **Tu t'es fait passer un sapin Paul, t'as payé le double de ce que ça vaut!**
> You got taken for a ride Paul, you paid twice what that thing's worth!

Sauté,e Nuts, cuckoo.

> **Notre professeur de français est sauté.**
> Our French teacher is cuckoo.

Sauter aux yeux (lit. *to jump in one's eyes*) To be obvious.

> **Ça saute aux yeux!**
> It's as plain as the nose on your face!

Savoir To know **Je le savais!** I knew it!

Semaine *f* **Dans la semaine des quatre jeudis!** (lit. *when there's a week with four Thursdays*) Never! Not in a million years!

> **Quand est-ce que Guy va arrêter de fumer? — Dans la semaine des quatre jeudis!**
> When is Guy going to quit smoking? — Never!

Séraphin *m* Cheapskate, tightwad.

Québec's answer to Dickens' Scrooge, *Séraphin* is the name of a miserly old soul from a book and TV story that for several decades

139

Séraphin Scrooge

captured the imagination of the Québec public. Set in pioneer days, the story and character were the creation of Québec author Claude-Henri Grignon in his novel *Un homme et son péché*, 1933, which was later adapted and aired on radio and TV from 1939 through 1970. With all this exposure, *Séraphin* naturally made its way into popular lingo as a colourful name for any humbug who pinched his pennies.

T'es un vrai Séraphin!
You're a real Scrooge!

While no longer on the air, our man has been immortalized in a little Laurentian town north of Montréal. Sainte-Adèle is the place, and its old-time *village de Séraphin* tells it all. With the TV character out of sight and out of mind, the expression too has faded from the collective conscience, and the standard term *avare* is now more often heard.

Reference: Trésors de la langue française au Québec

Smatte [smat] (inf.) (from Engl. *smart*) Nice, smart.

Faire son smatte To be a smart aleck, to show off.

Louis fait son smatte.
Louis is being a smart aleck.

Sortir avec To go out with.

Henri sort avec les gars une fois par semaine.
Henry goes out with the boys once a week.

Sortir dans les bars (lit. *to go out into the bars*) To go bar hopping.

On va sortir dans les bars à Montréal ce soir.
We're going bar hopping in Montréal tonight.

141

Sous *m* (lit. *pennies*) Money (in pocket), change.

> **J'ai pas assez de sous pour acheter ça.**
> I don't have enough money on me to buy that.

See ARGENT

Souper See DÉJEUNER

Spécial,e (lit. *special*) Different, something else, really something.

> **La cuisine de ma femme est spéciale.**
> My wife's cooking is different.

> **Cet acteur est spécial!**
> That actor is really something!

Super! Great!

> **C'est super!**
> That's great!

Other superlatives commonly heard in Québec in the sense of *great* are **Au boutte!** Écœurant!** (iron.) **Épouvantable!** (iron.) **Excellent! Extraordinaire! Fantastique! Formidable! Numéro un! Première classe! Terrible!** (iron.) and **Trippant!**

> **C'est extraordinaire!**
> It's great!

> **C'est numéro un!**
> That's just fine!

142

C'est trippant!
Far out!

Terrib'e terrib'e!   See L
Out of sight man!

More typical of European French to express the same exaltation and sometimes heard in Québec are *épatant, génial* and *chouette*. They are to Québec French what *jolly good!* and *smashing!* are to Canadian English.

Sûr C'est sûr! For sure! You bet!

Aimes-tu voyager? — C'est sûr!
Do you like to travel? — That's for sure!

T

Tannant,e Annoying, a pain.

> **Elle est tannante!**
> She's a pain in the neck!

Tanné,e Fed up.

> **Je suis tanné!**
> I'm fed up!

See VOYAGE

Tant mieux! So much the better! That's good!

Tant pis! Too bad!

Tantôt À tantôt! (may repl. *à tout à l'heure*) See you later!

T'as [taw] (short form of *tu as*) You have.

> **T'as un bel accent.**
> You've got a nice accent.

See T'ES

Téléphone *m* (lit. *telephone*) (may repl. *appel*) Call.

> **J'attends un téléphone.**
> I'm waiting for a call.

Température *f* (lit. *temperature*) (may repl. *temps*) Weather.

> **Quelle température fait-il?**
> What's the weather like?

> **La température est belle.**
> The weather's nice.

Temps *m* Time **Dans le temps de le dire!** (lit. *as fast as you can say it*) Before you can say Jack Robinson! Quick as a wink!

> **Je l'aurai fini dans le temps de le dire!**
> I'll have it finished before you can say Jack Robinson!

Tenter (lit. *to tempt*) To feel like.

> **Ça me tente d'écouter du jazz.**
> I feel like listening to some jazz.

See GOÛT

Tenue *f* Dress, attire **Tenue de soirée** From dressy to formal evening attire. **Tenue sport** Casual dress (jeans, etc.); not to be confused with **Tenue de sport** Sportswear or sports outfit.

See HABILLER

Terrasse *f* Outdoor café, sidewalk café.

In true French tradition, *les terrasses* abound in the main cities of Québec. This Québec ambiance à la française thrives in quarters such as *rue Saint-Denis, rue Prince-Arthur, rue Cresent* and *place Jacques-Cartier* (Montréal) and *la Grande Allée, rue Cartier* and *la basse-ville* (Québec City). They're an idyllic place to sit back and watch the Québécois world go by. And with the cosy table arrangement, you'll be practically sitting on your neighbour's lap, leaving no excuse whatsoever for not speaking the language of Laurier, or at least training your French ear.

T'es [tay] (short form of *tu es*) You are. Widely heard in conversation.

> **T'es belle!**
> You're beautiful!

See T'AS

Tête de linotte *f* (lit. *bird head*) Birdbrain.

> **C'est une vraie tête de linotte!**
> He/she's a real birdbrain!

Ti [tsee] (inf.) (short form of *petit*) Little. Used to form nicknames similar to *Johnny* and *Danny boy*. It goes well with certain names, e.g., *Ti-Claude, Ti-Guy, Ti-Jacques, Ti-Jean*.

See P'TIT; TS

Tiens, tiens! Well, well! Fancy that!

146

Terrasse
Outdoor, sidewalk café

Toé [twoy] ** (var. of *toi*) You.

> **Eh toé là!**
> Hey you!

See MOÉ

Toi C'est bien toi! (lit. *it's really you*) It's just like you!

> **Excuse-moi, Brigitte, mais j'ai encore oublié notre anniver-saire. — C'est bien toi Jacques!**
> I'm sorry Bridget, but I forgot our anniversary again. — That's just like you Jack!

Tomates *f* (lit. *tomatoes*) Money, bucks.

> **Ça m'a coûté deux cents tomates!**
> It cost me $200 bucks!

See ARGENT

Tomber sur les nerfs (lit. *to fall on one's nerves*) To get on one's nerves.

> **Ce bruit me tombe sur les nerfs.**
> That noise gets on my nerves.

Touche *f* (lit. *touch*) Puff, drag.

> **Donne-moi une touche de ta cigarette.**
> Give me a drag of your cigarette.

Touche du bois! Touch wood! (for good luck).

148

Tour *m* 1. Way, knack **Avoir le tour avec** To have a way with.

> **Mon grand-père avait le tour avec les chevaux.**
> My grandfather had a way with horses.

Avoir le tour pour To have a knack for.

> **Catherine a le tour pour apprendre des langues.**
> Cathy has a knack for learning languages.

2. Visit, outing **Faire un tour** To visit, to go for a walk, ride or drive.

> **Je vais faire un tour chez Marguerite.**
> I'm going over to Margy's.

> **Gérard est sorti faire un tour.**
> Gerry's gone out for a walk.

> **Nous avons fait un tour dans les Cantons de l'est.**
> We went for a drive in the Eastern Townships.

3. Trick **Jouer un tour à quelqu'un** To fool someone, to play a trick on someone.

> **Tu me joues un tour, hein?**
> Trying to fool me, eh?

See FARCE

Toutte [tuut] ** (var. of *tout*) All, everything.

> **Est-ce qu'elle t'a tout raconté? — Ouais, toutte!**
> Did she tell you everything? — Yep, everything!

149

Tout cuit Avoir tout cuit (dans le bec) (lit. *to have something completely cooked and placed right in your beak*) To be waited on hand and foot, to be spoonfed (students, for example).

> **Puis tu veux avoir tout cuit dans le bec, hein?**
> So you want to be waited on hand and foot do you?

Tournée des grands-ducs *f* (lit. *tour of the Grand Dukes*) Night on the town, grand tour.

A popular French expression from the late 18th century, after the Grand Dukes of Russia and their well-known fancy for high living out on the town. Now a Québec French favourite.

> **Ils vont faire la tournée des grands-ducs pour sa fête.**
> They're taking him out for a big night on the town for his birthday.

> **Avez-vous aimé votre tournée des grands-ducs à Paris?**
> Did you enjoy your grand tour of Paris?

Trente-six Se mettre sur son trente-six (lit. *to put on one's thirty six*) To get all dressed up, to get all decked out.

> **Les Québécois se mettent sur leur trente-six pour aller à la Place des Arts.**
> Québecers get all decked out to go to Place des Arts.

Trotter (lit. *to trot*) To be on the go.

> **Marcel trotte tous les jours.**
> Marcel's on the go every day.

La tournée des grands-ducs
(The tour of the Grand Dukes)
A big night on the town, a grand tour

See Tournée

Ts The Québécois pronunciation of the consonant *t* before the vowels *i* and *u*.

> **Viens-tu Michel?** [tsew]
> Are you coming Mike?
>
> **Tirez!** [tseer-ay]
> Pull!

See ZZZZZ

T'sais [tsay] (inf.) (short form of *tu sais*) You know, you see.

> **J'ai déménagé à Montréal, t'sais, pour trouver de l'ouvrage.**
> I moved to Montréal, you see, to find work.

Tu You. Creates a new, informal, interrogative form when added to a direct question. This form is very popular in Québec and can easily confuse the second-language débutant who ventures out of the classroom into the world of everyday French conversation.

You may hear:

C'est-tu fermé?	instead of	**Est-ce fermé?** Is it closed?
On y va-tu?	instead of	**On y va?** Shall we go?
Il fait-tu beau?	instead of	**Est-ce qu'il fait beau?** Is the weather nice?

U

V

Vaillant,e (lit. *valiant*, like the knights of old) Hard-working.

> **T'as fait tout ce travail? Que t'es vaillant!**
> You did all that work? Boy are you hard-working!

Valeur *f* **C'est de valeur!** (lit. *it's of value*) (may repl. *c'est dommage*) It's too bad!

Vas [vaw] (inf.) (from the verb *aller*) (var. of first person singular — *vais*) Going.

> **Je vas à Rivière-du-Loup.**
> I'm going to Rivière-du-Loup.

Vas-y! Go ahead! Go for it!

> **Vas-y Savard! Lance!**
> Go for it Savard! Shoot the puck!

Venir S'en venir (carrying on the tradition of 17th-century French and the language of playwright Molière) (may repl. *arriver*) To be coming, to be on its way.

> **L'autobus s'en vient.**
> The bus is coming.

Viens-t'en! Come here! Come along!

See ALLER, S'EN

Vent *m* **Quel bon vent t'amène?** (lit. *what good wind brings you here*) To what do we owe the pleasure of your visit?

Vie *f* **Qu'est-ce que tu fais dans la vie?** (lit. *what do you do in life*) What do you do for a living?

La belle vie! The good life!

Vieille fille *f* (lit. *old girl*) Female counterpart of VIEUX GARÇON.

Vieux garçon *m* (lit. *old boy*) 1. Bachelor. 2. A male who is either set in his ways, old-fashioned, inflexible in his way of thinking or downright childish. You'll hear:

> **C'est un vieux garçon!**
> **Il fait vieux garçon!**
> **Ça fait vieux garçon!**

See VIEILLE FILLE

154

Vin *m* **Mettre de l'eau dans son vin** To put water in one's wine, to be conciliatory or tactful.

> **Le médiateur a dit, et à la direction, et aux employés, de mettre de l'eau dans leur vin.**
> The mediator told both the management and the employees to be conciliatory.

Visite *f* **Avoir de la grande visite** To have a special visit.

> **Ah, de la grande visite!**
> Wow, look who's come to visit!

Vite sur ses patins (lit. *fast on one's skates*) Quick thinking, quick to act.

> **Luc est vite sur ses patins.**
> Luke is quick as a whip. Luke is very fast.

Vivable Livable, suitable for living in or with (place, person).

> **C'est vivable ici.**
> This place is livable.

> **Mon mari est pas vivable!**
> My husband is unbearable!

V'là [vlaw] (inf.) (short form of *voilà*) There is, there are.

> **V'là Joseph!**
> There's Joe!

Luc est vite sur ses patins!
(*Luke is fast on his skates*)
Boy is Luke fast!

See Vite

Vous autres (lit. *you others*) (inf.) (may repl. *vous*) You, you guys.

> **Eh vous autres, attendez-moi!**
> Hey you guys, wait for me!

See NOUS AUTRES

Vous vs. Tu to say *you* in the singular. Should one say, for example, *comment allez-vous?* or *comment vas-tu?* to ask *how are you?*

Indeed, you'll be speaking French in Québec with many a different person in many a different place. And each time you do, you'll have to choose between *vous* and *tu* in the way you address them. Well, it's an age-old decision that even native French speakers weary of making, because *vous* can be too formal and put people at a distance, while *tu* may offend when it seems overly familiar.

But not to despair or pull out your hair! All you need do is remember two easy RULES:

- *Tu* is for children, teens and people you know well (especially family).

- *Vous* is used for everyone else, including customers, waiters, bus drivers, and bosses (unless you really get to know them).

Then keep in mind that in Québec the rules are more relaxed. The new people you meet will call you *tu* almost right away, whereas francophones from abroad will use *vous* indefinitely or until they really get to know you. And total strangers in Québec may be addressed as *tu* in some situations: at sports clubs, parties and other social occasions, *tu* is friendly and *vous* verbose!

For you, the budding bilinguist, however, life's a bowl of cherries. As a non-francophone, you enjoy a wide margin of error — francophones know you're trying and won't take offence should you happen to misaddress them. *Vive la tolérance!*

See MADAME, MADEMOISELLE, MONSIEUR

Voyage *m* **Avoir son voyage** (lit. *to have one's trip*) To be astonished, or exasperated, depending on the case.

> **Ben, j'ai mon voyage!**
> Well, now I've seen everything! *or*
> I've had it up to here!

> See TANNÉ; REVENIR

Voyons! 1. What's this! How in the heck!

Something people mutter to themselves on encountering a snag in whatever it is they're trying to do, from removing a stubborn spot on clothing to trying to make a bum computer program work. It's a kind of non-swearword that does the same job.

2. Same as VOYONS DONC.

Voyons donc! Come on! Look here! Don't be silly!

> **Tu prends trop de place, pousse-toi. — Voyons donc!**
> You're taking too much room, shove over. — Look here!

> **Est-ce que je te dérange? — Voyons donc, pas du tout!**
> Am I disturbing you? — Don't be silly, not at all!

> See ARRÊTE DONC

Vrai Pas vrai! (lit. *not true*) No kidding! You're kidding!

> **On va faire du rafting sur la rivière Rouge cet été.**
> **— Pas vrai!**
> We're going white-water rafting on the Rouge River this summer.
> — You're kidding!

158

Voyons!
How in the heck!

Vue *f* (lit. *view*) (may repl. *film*) Movie.

> **Il y avait une bonne vue à la télé hier.**
> There was a good movie on the TV yesterday.

> **Vas-tu aux vues ce soir?**
> Are you going to the movies tonight?

W

Wa-sh! See OUACHE

Wise (inf.) (from Engl., same pron.) Able to handle oneself, resourceful, street wise.

> **Inquiète-toi pas pour elle, c'est une fille ben wise.**
> Don't worry about her, she can take care of herself just fine.

Wô les moteurs! Hold on! Hold your horses!

X

Y

Y [ee] A short form pronunciation of *il* (he, it) and *ils* (they).

Y parle anglais.
He speaks English.

Y faut dans son domaine.
It's a must in his line of work.

Y sont bilingues.
They're bilingual.

This soft-sounding *y* in place of *il* [eel] is a standard feature of natural, everyday speech, and you'll hear it frequently. You'll also see the written symbol *y* on billboard ads and other places where spoken French is visually represented. Another notation is *i*. While not generally indicated in the examples in this book, *y* is a possible pronunciation wherever *il* and *ils* occur.

Y is employed by Québécois speakers in both formal and informal conversation, with a few full *il*'s occurring naturally from time to time. The only francophones who pronounce their *il*'s with all the *l*s ringing loud and clear are TV and radio newscasters, who, like their CBC and other broadcasting counterparts in English Canada, wax a more textbook style of speech.

See L

Yeux *m* **Faire des beaux yeux** (lit. *to make beautiful eyes*) To give someone a nice smile, or to make eyes at someone for real flirting or flirting in a "just kidding" sort of way.

161

Youppie! [yoo-pee] Yippee!

> **Youppie! Les écoles sont fermées aujourd'hui.**
> Yippee! The schools are closed today.

Z

Zzzzz A distinctive and easy-to-hear colouring of the letter *d* in Québécois French, occurring before the vowels *i* and *u*.

> **Ma chère Diane.** [dzee-an]
> Dear Diane.

> **C'est pas si dur.** [dzewr]
> It's not that hard.

See TS

BIBLIOGRAPHY

Barbaud, Philippe. 1984. *Le choc des patois en Nouvelle-France*. Sillery: Presses de l'Université du Québec.

Barbaud, Philippe. 1987. *Le français sans façon*. Montréal: Éditions Hurtubise.

Beauchemin, Normand. 1982. *Dictionnaire d'expressions figurées en français parlé du Québec. Les 700 québécoiseries les plus usuelles*. Sherbrooke: Université de Sherbrooke.

Belisle, Louis-Alexandre. 1979. *Dictionnaire nord-américain de la langue française*. Montréal: Beauchemin.

Bergeron, Léandre. 1980. *Dictionnaire de la langue québécoise*. Montréal: VLB Éditeur.

Bergeron, Léandre. 1982. *The Québécois Dictionary*. Toronto: Lorimer.

Centre Éducatif et Culturel. 1987. *Dictionnaire du français plus*. Montréal.

Charest, Gilles. 1980. *Sacres et blasphèmes québécois*. Montréal: Québec-Amérique.

Clapin, Sylva. 1894. *Dictionnaire canadien-français*. Sainte-Foy: Presses de l'Université Laval (1974).

Collins — Société du Nouveau Littré. 1978. *Collins-Robert French-English, English-French Dictionary*. London-Paris.

Corbeil, Jean-Claude, and Louis Guilbert. September 1976. *Langue française — Le français au Québec*. Periodical. Paris: Larousse.

Desbiens, Jean-Paul. 1960. *Les insolences du frère Untel*. Montréal: Éditions de l'Homme.

DesRuisseaux, Pierre. 1978. *Le livre des proverbes québécois*. Montréal: Hurtubise HMH.

Dunn, Oscar. 1880. *Glossaire franco-canadien*. Sainte-Foy: Presses de l'Université Laval (1976).

Gale Research Company. 1983. *Idioms and Phrases Index*. Detroit.

Government of Canada, Public Service Commission — Language Training. 1973. *La Parlure*. Ottawa.

Groupe de recherche, l'Université de Laval, Lionel Boisvert [et al]. 1985. *Trésors de la langue française au Québec, dictionnaire du français québécois*. Sainte-Foy: Presses de l'Université Laval.

Hurtig Publishers. 1985. *The Canadian Encyclopedia*. Edmonton.

Lafleur, Bruno. 1979. *Dictionnaire des locutions idiomatiques françaises*. Montréal: Éditions du Renouveau pédagogique.

Lexicographic Research Centre, Université de Montréal. 1962. *The Canadian Dictionary*. Toronto: McClelland and Stewart.

Lexicographical Centre for Canadian English, University of Victoria, B.C. 1967. *A Dictionary of Canadianisms*. Toronto: W.J. Gage.

Librairie Larousse. 1977. *Grand Larousse de la langue française*. Paris.

Orkin, Mark. 1967. *Speaking Canadian French*. Revised edition. Toronto: General Publishing.

Ouellet, Jo. 1966. *Instant French — Expo 67 Montréal*. Toronto: Swann Publishing.

Normand, Pascal. 1981. *La chanson québécoise — miroir d'un peuple*. Montréal: France-Amérique.

Proteau, Lorenzo. 1982. *La parlure québécoise*. Boucherville: Proteau.

Robert, Paul. 1979. *Le Petit Robert*. Paris: Société du Nouveau Littré.

Robinson, Sinclair, and Donald Smith. 1984. *Practical Handbook of Québec and Acadian French*. Toronto: Anansi.

Rodriguez, Liliane. 1984. *Mots d'hier, mots d'aujourd'hui*. Saint-Boniface (Manitoba): Les Éditions des plaines.

Rogers, David. 1977. *Dictionnaire de la langue québécoise rurale*. Montréal: VLB Éditeur.

Société du parler français au Canada. 1930. *Glossaire du parler français au Canada*. Sainte-Foy: Presses de l'Université Laval (1968).

University of Toronto. Edited by Helmut Kallmann, Gilles Potvin and Kenneth Winters. 1981. *Encyclopedia of Music in Canada*. Toronto: University of Toronto Press.

Wade, Mason. 1956. *The French Canadians, 1760-1945*. Toronto: MacMillan.

Wade, Mason. 1968. *The French Canadians, 1760-1967, Volume II, 1911-1967*. Toronto: MacMillan.

Walker, Douglas. 1984. *The Pronunciation of Canadian French*. Ottawa: University of Ottawa Press.

COMMENTS

Please convey any comments about **French Fun** to Steve Timmins, c/o Northwinds Press, P.O. Box 391, Beloeil, Québec, J3G 5S9.

Veuillez communiquer tout commentaire à Steve Timmins a/s Les éditions Vents du Nord, C.P. 391, Beloeil, Québec, J3G 5S9.

TO ORDER ADDITIONAL COPIES OF THIS BOOK:

POUR COMMANDER DES EXEMPLAIRES ADDITIONNELS DE CE LIVRE:

Call/*Appeler* **(514) 467-0654**